The Greater Wilmington Chamber of Commerce is pleased to bring to Wilmington this book entitled, *Wilmington: A Pictorial History*. This beautifully illustrated and carefully documented volume will prove a valuable addition to your family library and a rare collector's item in years to come.

We gratefully acknowledge the work of Anne Russell, author of this book, for her commitment to this publication. We express our appreciation to those who assisted her and to the families, individuals and their descendants who made this history.

In the spirit of community awareness and family relationships we dedicate this book to the citizens of Wilmington—past, present and future.

Officers, Directors, and Staff

Greater Wilmington
Chamber of Commerce

WILMINGTON
250
YEARS

A Pictorial History
WILM

DONNING PUBLISHING COMPANY
Design by Randolph Bruce

INGTON

By ANNE RUSSELL

South Third Street looking north toward Market Street, circa 1900. Courtesy of James Alfred Miller, Jr.

First Printing 1981
Revised Edition 1989

Library of Congress Cataloging in Publication Data

Russell, Anne.
    Wilmington: a pictorial history.

    Bibliography: P.
    Includes index.
    1. Wilmington, N.C.—Description—Views.
2. Wilmington, N.C.—History—Pictorial works.
I. Title.
F264.W7R73   975.627   80-22633
ISBN 0-89865-055-0 (pbk.)

Printed in the United States of America

This view of Wilmington during the Civil War was drawn by a newspaper artist on February 27, 1865, just after the city was occupied by Federal troops. Released Yankee prisoners file down South Front Street and turn the corner at Dock Street to reach ships which will take them home. Included in the drawing are the Federal fleet, the Customs House, and the Town Hall. Courtesy of the *Wilmington Star-News.*

CONTENTS

The oldest known outdoor photograph taken in North Carolina was by an unidentified photographer who captured this view of Market Street around 1847 looking east from the Cape Fear River toward Third Street, past the Burgwyn-Wright House and St. James Episcopal Church, with a glimpse of the four-story Hill-Wootten residence on the far right. Courtesy of Amon Carter Museum, Fort Worth, Texas.

FOREWORD

Robert Frost wrote that we were the land's before the land was ours. So it was with Wilmington. Its history is long—its people were colonials, and much of America's history has been Wilmington's history.

In the broad sweep and panoramic vision, eras can be marked in time. Yet there is a timeless quality to this city on a river and near the sea, and both river and sea are large parts of the portrait.

Here, then, is the portrait of a city, a portrait made from many moments whose magic was caught and frozen in time and thus became timeless. These pictures became frozen moments which move again and live again for those who turn the pages and are caught in the unfolding of history.

Anne Russell looked at and studied hundreds and hundreds of pictures before selecting the 350 or more which make up this remarkable portrait of a remarkable city. To the pictures she has added a concise text which relates the story of Wilmington and the lower Cape Fear region from the first recorded beginnings—the explorations of Verrazano and Ayllon in the early half of the sixteenth century, through the chartering of Newtown (Wilmington) in 1739, the colonial years and the years from then to now, in 1981.

It is a story of a place and a people, both fascinating and indelibly fixed in a sweep of eras and of time itself.

Wilmington's history, its character and its charm are captured here in a splendid achievement.

SAM RAGAN

PREFACE

Throughout my life, as I have lived in many cities in many different states, I have returned to Wilmington, North Carolina, for sustenance, for Wilmington to me is home. It is a very special place where the air is soft with salt moisture, the trees are hung with gray moss and ornamented with creamy magnolias, the fiery azalea and variegated hydrangea bloom, the sun rises over the ocean and sets beyond the river, the sandy earth is strewn with huge pine cones and sprightly gaillardia, the falls are golden, the winters are mild, the springs are sweet, and the summers are filled with frolic. Wilmington is oyster roasts, swimming, sailing, bare feet, and long, slow walks down plaza-lined streets. In Wilmington I can hear the voices of my ancestors whispering in high-ceilinged rooms and on wind-swept sounds and beaches.

Lying between two bodies of water, the Cape Fear River and the Atlantic Ocean, bordered by sounds and marshes, dotted with lakes and ponds, crisscrossed by streams, decorated with fountains, soaked by northeasters and hurricanes, Wilmington might well have been born under the sign of Aquarius. Indeed, it was incorporated in Aquarian February, in 1740. From the port of Wilmington's amniotic waters, the state of North Carolina has drawn life. Its proximity to river and sea has made it a center of commerce, so that by 1790 it was the most populous city in the state.

The people of Wilmington came from strong stock from a potpourri of ethnic groups. Indians, Negroes, Scots, Jews, the English, the Irish, the French, Germans, the Dutch, the Swiss, Poles, Hungarians, Austrians, Russians, Italians, and Greeks gave of their skills to build the city which exists today. Although I have always loved Wilmington, my research for this book has given me a new respect for its ecology, the way in which each individual, family, race or nationality, industry, event fits into the entirety, all necessary pieces of the whole. The many nuances of Wilmington, its lovely ambience, derive from this rich variety.

At its origins in the 1700s, Wilmington was a serious, hard-working settlement. In its heyday in the 1800s, it was boastful, prideful, self-important. In the 1920s, it was frivolous. In the 1930s, it was unified against adversity. In the 1950s, it slipped into a somnambulistic loss of pace; and in the 1960s and 1970s, it rediscovered its pride, restoring its historic district, attracting new residents and industry. The Wilmington panorama stimulates a sense of heritage in those born within its boundaries and a sense of excitement in newcomers and visitors, making us wish to remain a lifetime here, or at the least, to come to visit again and again.

The Orton Hotel was constructed on Front Street in 1888 by Colonel K.M. Murchison, who named it for his Orton Plantation. Until 1949, the Orton Hotel was the site of many important events. The main lobby was often filled with traveling salesmen, and women guests used the side entrance where there was a mirrored and red-carpeted sitting room. John, the porter from the Atlantic Coast Line Railroad Station, and Polite, the headwaiter, were popular with the guests. The hotel was destroyed by fire. Courtesy of the North Carolina Collection, UNC Library, Chapel Hill.

ACKNOWLEDGMENTS

This pictorial history of Wilmington was made possible by the private and public, amateur and professional, known and unknown photographers who have sought to capture the city's people, buildings, landscape and events at special moments in time. The services of photographer Tom Prestia and the UNC-Wilmington physics department photo lab have been indispensable in reproducing these efforts. The archives of the New Hanover Public Library, the New Hanover County Museum, the Lower Cape Fear Historical Society, the University of North Carolina Library at Chapel Hill, the State of North Carolina, the *Wilmington Star-News*, the *Wilmington Journal*, and *Scene* magazine provided much valuable material.

Janet Seapker, director of the New Hanover County Museum, read the manuscript for accuracy and made helpful suggestions throughout the project. Bob Davis, former director of the Lower Cape Fear Council for the Arts, made connections. Dr. Melton McLaurin of the UNC-Wilmington history department, R. V. Asbury of the Historic Wilmington Foundation, Tom Jervay of the *Wilmington Journal*, and Joe Nesbitt of the *Wilmington Star-News* gave many hours of their time, as did Katherine Howell of the New Hanover County Library.

Jerry Cotten of the UNC-Chapel Hill Library, Dick Lankford of the North Carolina State Archives, Bobbie Marcroft and Joe Stanley of *Scene* magazine, photographer Herbert Howard, Tony Rivenbark of Thalian Hall, Bob Warren of the Lower Cape Fear Historical Society, and historians Bill Reaves and Dr. Hubert Eaton gave generous assistance. Photographic consultant Elizabeth Russell, genealogist James Miller, and authors Crockette Hewlett, Lewis Hall, and William Whitehead were a great help.

The collections of Ida Kellam, Howard Loughlin, Emma MacMillan, Louis Moore, Dr. Robert Fales, Felice Sadgwar and Mabel Manly, Mary Wootten, Beulah Meier, and the Wilmington Junior League were important sources of material, as were the books of Andrew Howell, James Sprunt and W. W. Storm. The recollections of Amoret Wootten Davis, Elizabeth Franks, Franklin Block, Adrian Hurst, Billy Hurst, Al Miller and J. Bradford Wiggins were equally of value.

This book could not have been put together without the firm foundation of the aforementioned historians who painfully researched and transcribed their own special areas of knowledge. It is hoped that while this one volume cannot possibly cover in depth all of the 250 years of Wilmington history, it may synthesize and portray in pictures the people, places and events so well documented to date and add some new insights. Deep appreciation goes to Howard Reed Garriss, Jennifer Twiggs, Mary Catherine Twiggs, and Leila Garriss, who kept the home fires burning while *Wilmington: A Pictorial History* was in process.

The Old Dram Tree stood in Wilmington harbor where the Cape Fear River takes a sharp bend. For centuries the moss-covered cypress served as a channel sentinel welcoming incoming sailors and bidding outgoing sailors farewell. On outward voyages, by the time the aged tree was reached the ship was under full sail, and the first drink or "dram" was given the sailors. By the same token, on inward voyages the sailors were served a last "dram" before lowering the sails. From a private collection; courtesy of *Scene* magazine.

INTRODUCTION

Popular history generally comes in narrative form. *Wilmington: A Pictorial History*, by Anne Russell, is evidence that the manner of presentation need not be so narrowly confined. The volume also gives support to the old adage, "One picture is worth more than ten thousand words." This accomplishment has been made possible because The Donning Company/Publishers has included Wilmington in the impressive list of community histories it is in the process of telling by means of pictures.

The choice of Wilmington is a worthy one. Approaching its 250th anniversary, it was founded in 1734, just eight years after the coming of settlers to the Cape Fear River had given North Carolina its first harbor suitable for overseas trade. In addition to becoming the metropolitan center of the area, it also became, and continues to be, the principal seaport of North Carolina. In 1740 it was incorporated and was, until the early 1900s, the largest town in the state.

In many ways the development of Wilmington has followed the same pattern as other Southern coastal cities such as Charleston and Savannah. As a seaport, its commercial life focused on the river and its shipping, which ranged from large overseas vessels to small local craft. Until roads were built, and railroads came much later, the inhabitants depended almost altogether on water for transportation. The vessels from afar were vital to trade, and they brought to the community an air of excitement and sophistication, but there were few if any craft more colorful than the local commercial steamers which carried passengers and cargo along the river until the 1930s.

From the beginning the Cape Fear people depended to a large extent on forest products, and throughout the colonial period, more naval stores in the form of pine tar, pitch, and turpentine were shipped out of the Cape Fear than from any other port in the British Empire. After the Revolution the export of these stores was resumed, but turpentine became the most important product and continued to be until the beginning of the present century. Cotton then became the principal export for several decades, but in recent years Wilmington's shipping has become increasingly diverse and its port facilities vastly improved.

Normally, life in Wilmington through the years has been pleasant and tranquil, but there have been times of tumult and of historical importance. One such occasion was the anti-Stamp Tax demonstration of the 1760s, which contributed to the coming of the American Revolution. Later, when the conflict came, the town was occupied for some time by the British army, under General Cornwallis. From there he marched to Virginia and to eventual defeat at Yorktown. It was during the Civil War, however, that the spotlight of history shone brightest on Wilmington. As one of the important seaports of the Confederacy, it was a center of operations for the fast, sleek vessels that slipped through the Union blockade with vitally needed food and supplies from abroad. From Wilmington they were sent on by train to the forces in the field, especially to Lee in Virginia.

During the war years Wilmington bustled with unusual activity which increased near the end of the conflict when it became the last Confederate port to remain open. Its end came when Fort Fisher, which protected the entrance to the river, fell to the Union in January 1865. The occupation of Wilmington followed, and in April, cut off from aid from the outside world, Lee surrendered, and the Confederacy collapsed.

The publishers did well in selecting Dr. Russell for this volume. In addition to her sound, scholarly qualifications, she has a "feel" for the subject matter that is based on roots that go deep into Wilmington's past. She has sought out and found in various collections a wealth of Wilmington photographs. From them she has carefully selected some 350 which include a well-balanced mixture of people, places, structures, things, and events. Each photograph has an explanatory caption, and the whole is brought together by a succinct and informative chronological narrative. The story she tells is a broad one, yet contains sufficient details to give desired life and warmth. From this volume the reader will gain both pleasure and knowledge, a combination that is not always easy to come by.

LAWRENCE LEE

Wilmington was named in
honor of Spencer Compton,
Earl of Wilmington, 1673-
1743. Courtesy of the North
Carolina State Archives.

COLONIAL ERA

Wilmington was incorporated in February 1740 by an act of the North Carolina General Assembly. Named in honor of Spencer Compton, the Earl of Wilmington and patron of Royal Governor Gabriel Johnston, the town had been called New Carthage, New Liverpool, New Town and Newton. Many Wilmington streets were named after streets in Liverpool, England, among them: Red Cross, Castle, Walnut, Chestnut, Princess, Market, Dock, Orange, Ann, Nun, Queen, and Church streets.

The early exploration of the Cape Fear region by Giovanni da Verrazano caused him to describe it as "open Countrey rising in height above the sandie shoare with many faire fields and plaines, full of mightie great woods, some very thicke, and some thinne, replenished with divers sorts of trees, as pleasant and delectable to behold, as is possible to imagine." The name of the region meant "awesome cape."

Queen Elizabeth opened the way for English colonization, and William Hilton was sent to the area in 1663. The Cape Fear Indians and the pirates, including Stede Bonnet, impeded settlement for fifty years. In 1729, the New Hanover precinct was created by the North Carolina General Assembly. In 1735, Roger Haynes was granted land now called Castle Hayne and Richard Eagles was granted what is now Eagles Island. In 1740, the town and township of Wilmington was approved. St. James Parish was divided, with land deeded for St. James Church, and the area west of the river becoming St. Philips Parish. St. Philips Church was near the Town of Brunswick, which had been designated as a port of trade prior to the founding of Wilmington. In these early days, a rivalry existed between Brunswick and Wilmington, with Brunswick's importance fading as Wilmington made progress.

As an official port of entry, Wilmington's primary sources of income were the shipping, lumber, naval stores, and rice industries. Culture was enhanced by the founding of the Cape Fear Library in the 1760s on Market Street between Front and Second streets. The newspaper *Cape Fear Gazette* appeared, and Colonel James Innes made a 1754 bequest in his will for a free school to be established upon his death. In 1765, Royal Governor William Tryon took the oath of office in Wilmington, with the Provincial Assembly meeting in town that same year. When the Stamp Act was passed in 1765 by the British Parliament, the people of Wilmington forced the Stamp Master, William Houston, to resign. A resistance group called the "Sons of Liberty" grew, and in 1766 Governor Tryon announced repeal of the hated act.

In 1774, a Committee of Safety was formed by Cornelius Harnett, William Hooper, John Quince, Francis Clayton, Robert Hogg, John Ancrum, Archibald Maclaine, John Robeson, and James Walker. In 1776, William Hooper signed the Declaration of Independence as a member of the Continental Congress. The mood of this period of Wilmington history was captured by Scotswoman Janet Schaw in her *Journal of A Lady of Quality.* Describing Wilmington during her visit to the area in 1774, Miss Schaw said, "This town lies low, but is not disagreeable. There is at each end of it an ascent, which is dignified with the title of the hills; on them are some very good houses. . . ."

The first decisive battle of the Revolution in North Carolina was fought at Moore's Creek Bridge near Wilmington on February 27, 1776, when revolutionary forces defeated the loyalists. In April 1781, General Charles Cornwallis occupied Wilmington with his troops for eighteen days. British troops were withdrawn from the town when Cornwallis surrendered at Yorktown in October 1781. The citizens of Wilmington luxuriated in their freedom, the 1,200 inhabitants and 150 houses taking on a more social aspect, and business enterprises flourished.

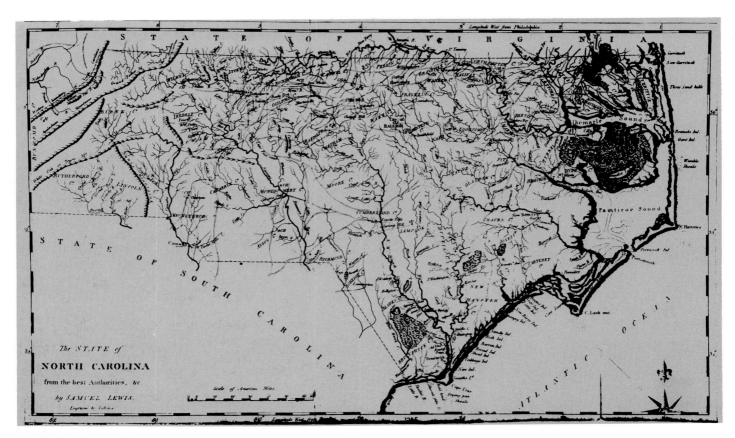

North Carolina as it appeared at the end of the eighteenth century. Wilmington is situated at the mouth of the Cape Fear River, the only major river in the state which flows directly into the Atlantic Ocean. From the *North Carolina Atlas.*

C. J. Sauthier's 1769 map of Wilmington shows many small buildings located near the Cape Fear River. Front Street, Second Street, Third Street and Fourth Street run horizontally, while Market Street runs vertically toward the top of the map, marked "Road to New Bern." St. James Church, the Courthouse, and the "Common Jail" are at the intersections of Market and Fourth Street, Market and Front Street, and Market and Third Street, respectively. Eagles Island is directly across the Cape Fear River from the town. At this time, a stocks, pillory, and public whipping post were at the site of the jail. In the absence of a fire department, fire was a constant threat to the wooden buildings, and residents were required to own fire buckets. A Market House, where produce and meat were sold, occupied the space below the Courthouse. Physicians, merchants, innkeepers, mariners, attorneys, craftsmen, and blacksmiths were occupants of the town. Courtesy of the North Carolina State Archives.

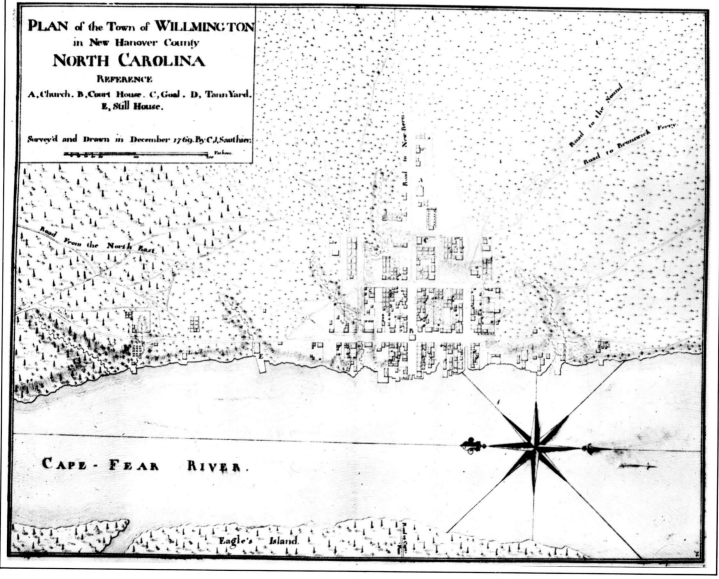

PLAN of the Town of WILLMINGTON in New Hanover County NORTH CAROLINA

REFERENCE

A, Church. B, Court House. C, Goal. D, Tann Yard. E, Still House.

Survey'd and Drawn in December 1769. By C. J. Sauthier.

CAPE - FEAR RIVER.

Eagle's Island.

This photograph of the interior of St. Philips Church at Brunswick shows the ruins of the building. Established in 1729 and completed in 1768, the church was struck by a severe summer storm in 1760. Lightning made a direct hit, and the roof collapsed under the torrential rains. When repairs were made, the finished church had walls three feet thick, a massive arched door, and a small belfry. Courtesy of the North Carolina State Archives.

This drawing of a North Carolina coastal Indian was made by John White, whose notable pictures of American Indians are in the British Museum. Courtesy of the Smithsonian Institution.

St. James Episcopal Church at the corner of Third and Market streets was begun as a parish in 1729. The original church was built in 1751 on land donated by Michael Higgins. In 1839, the present building was constructed on the property of Dr. A. J. deRosset. To raise funds for the building of the church in 1751, subscribers reserved space for family pews to be built, the space for each pew in proportion to the amount donated. Pews were passed down to succeeding generations by inheritance or were assigned by the owner. In contrast to the present church, the early church was a simple, square brick building with a peaked roof and no belfry. Courtesy of St. James Episcopal Church.

Historic St. James Church at the corner of Third and Market streets houses a famous painting of the head of Christ, *Ecce Homo* "Behold the Man," which is estimated to be over 500 years old. A portrait of Christ with a crown of thorns on his head and blood on his face and body, the painting was captured from a Spanish pirate ship in 1748 at a settlement on the Cape Fear River twenty miles below Wilmington. The artist who painted the portrait is unknown, although it is thought to be Francisco Pacheco, who lived in Spain in the sixteenth century. Courtesy of the North Carolina Collection, UNC Library, Chapel Hill.

The tombstone of Frances Wilkinson, who died at age eighteen on July 4, 1788, after the birth of her son William, who died when he was eight days old. The grave of Mrs. Wilkinson and her baby is in the St. James Churchyard at Fourth and Market streets. The historic graveyard predates Oakdale Cemetery, which was founded in 1855. Other downtown cemeteries included an old Indian burial ground at Fifth and Market streets and a Quaker graveyard at Fifth and Campbell streets. Courtesy of the North Carolina State Archives.

This photograph taken in the late 1800s shows the site of Governor William Tryon's residence at Russellboro, below Wilmington. The home outside of Brunswick Town was burned in 1776 by raiding parties conducted by British troops. Governor Tryon also had a residence on Market Street in Wilmington not far from the Cape Fear River. Here the North Carolina Legislature met in 1765, and Stamp Master William Houston resigned in that same year. Tryon continued in office and in residence in North Carolina until 1771. Courtesy of the North Carolina State Archives.

THIS PUBLIC AREA PERPETUATES THE NAME OF
COLONEL JAMES INNES
A FEARLESS AND BRAVE NEW HANOVER COUNTY SOLDIER,
HE SERVED AGAINST THE SPANISH FORCES AT CARTAGENA,
COLOMBIA, IN 1740, AND IN 1759 COMMANDED THE COLONIAL
FORCES IN THE FRENCH AND INDIAN WAR. IN THAT CAMPAIGN
HE MADE HIS WILL LEAVING A LARGE PART OF HIS CONSIDERABLE
FORTUNE "FOR THE USE OF A FREE SCHOOL FOR THE
BENEFIT OF THE YOUTH OF NORTH CAROLINA".

INNES ACADEMY-BELIEVED TO BE THE FIRST SCHOOL
IN THIS STATE FOR THE PURPOSE DESIGNATED,
WAS LOCATED ON THIS SITE IN 1783.

Innes Academy was established in 1783 and a school was opened in 1800 at Third and Princess streets where the City Hall and Thalian Hall now stand. The original trustees of Innes Academy were Samuel Ashe, Archibald Maclaine, William Hill, Thomas McGuire, John Ingram, John Hay, Edward Starkey, John Lillington and Robert Schaw. Colonel James Innes, commander of the Colonial forces in the French and Indian War, donated the property for the school. In 1804, Innes Academy was closed. Courtesy of the *Wilmington Star-News.*

John Burgwin, treasurer of the colony of Carolina, built the Burgwin-Wright House at the corner of Third and Market streets in 1770, also known as the Cornwallis House. The Hermitage, one of the great plantations of the Northeast Cape Fear River, was another home of John Burgwin. A copy of the Copley portrait, this photograph is from the Julian Martin Collection; courtesy of the Lower Cape Fear Historical Society.

The Burgwin-Wright House at the corner of Third and Market streets was once the site of the county jail. The property was purchased by Judge Joshua G. Wright, who added a wing to the house after it passed from the ownership of John Burgwin. Tradition has it that the house was the Wilmington headquarters of Lord Charles Cornwallis, commander of the British forces in 1781. During the Cornwallis occupancy, the story goes, a daughter of Judge Wright became friendly with a young British officer. With a diamond, the officer engraved his initials and those of the Wright daughter on a pane of glass in a window of the house, where they remained for many years. The house is now the headquarters of the North Carolina Society of Colonial Dames. Courtesy of the *Wilmington Star-News*.

The Hermitage, plantation home owned by John Burgwin, at Castle Hayne, north of Wilmington. The Hermitage burned in 1881. Photograph of an etching copied in *Magazine of American History*, Volume 16, 1886; courtesy of the North Carolina State Archives.

William Hooper, Wilmington lawyer who signed the Declaration of Independence as a member of the Continental Congress of 1776. The Masonic Lodge met at Hooper's residence at Masonboro Sound, called "Finian." Noted for his hospitality, Hooper was host to lawmakers and military officers, who found his home a quiet retreat. Courtesy of Crockette Hewlett, from a photograph of an oil portrait obtained from the North Carolina State Archives.

Finian was the Masonboro Sound residence of William Hooper, who bought 138 acres in 1773 for 165 pounds. Handmade bricks and oyster shell mortar were used in the porch-enclosed, two-story house. The house as it appears in this picture had become the property of Julia Parsley and Henry Peschau in 1914 and burned in 1931. An old Irish folksong from "Finian's Rainbow" captures the feeling of the gracious residence; "You will never grow old/ You will never grow poor/ If you look to the rainbow/ Beyond the next hill." Courtesy of Crockette Hewlett.

Finian as it appeared around 1900. Courtesy of the *Wilmington Star-News.*

The Cornelius Harnett monument was unveiled on Market Street at Fourth Street in 1907 as a memorial to the Wilmington patriot who served as president of the North Carolina Provincial Council and the Council of Safety until his election as a member of the Continental Congress in 1777. Harnett died in 1781 and is buried in St. James Churchyard. The inscription on his tomb reads: "Slave to no sect, he took no private road,/ But looked through nature up to Nature's God." Courtesy of the *Wilmington Star-News.*

The home of Cornelius Harnett at Negro Head Point, where the two branches of the Cape Fear River unite at Wilmington. The Colonial residence stood on a wooded bluff and was named Hilton after one of the explorers from Barbados who visited the Cape Fear in 1663. From the Julian Martin Collection; courtesy of the Lower Cape Fear Historical Society.

Hilton in a state of disrepair. The residence of the Hill family for a number of years, the house has been demolished. From the Julian Martin Collection; courtesy of the Lower Cape Fear Historical Society.

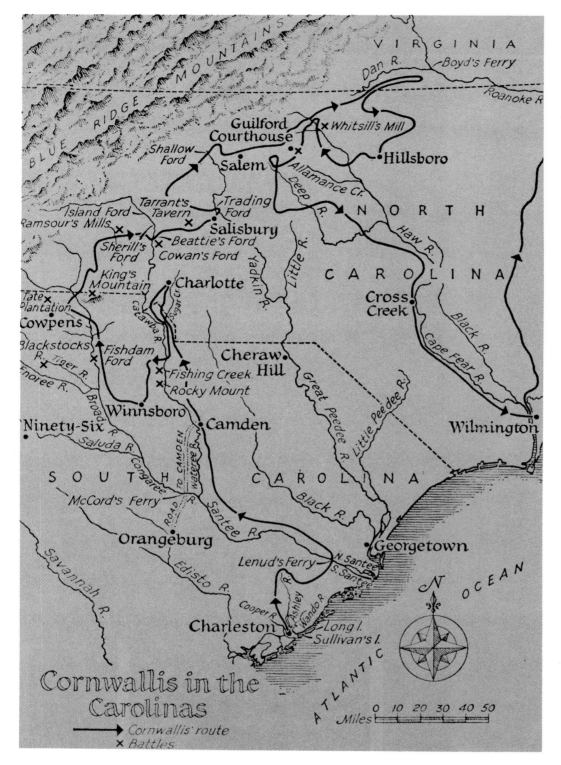

This map shows the route of General Lord Charles Cornwallis through the Carolinas during the Revolutionary War. Traveling along the Cape Fear River, Cornwallis reached Wilmington in April 1781, after his victory at Guilford Court House. Cornwallis made Wilmington his headquarters for eighteen days, living in the Burgwin-Wright House at the corner of Third and Market streets, with the British cavalry occupying St. James Church across the street as a "riding school." On April 25, Cornwallis left Wilmington to lead his troops to Virginia, where he soon met his fate at Yorktown. Courtesy of the North Carolina State Archives.

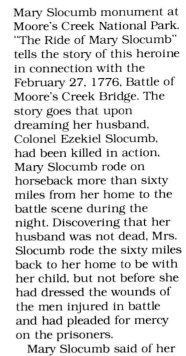

Mary Slocumb monument at Moore's Creek National Park. "The Ride of Mary Slocumb" tells the story of this heroine in connection with the February 27, 1776, Battle of Moore's Creek Bridge. The story goes that upon dreaming her husband, Colonel Ezekiel Slocumb, had been killed in action, Mary Slocumb rode on horseback more than sixty miles from her home to the battle scene during the night. Discovering that her husband was not dead, Mrs. Slocumb rode the sixty miles back to her home to be with her child, but not before she had dressed the wounds of the men injured in battle and had pleaded for mercy on the prisoners.

Mary Slocumb said of her ride, "I felt that it was only true womanly feeling which had caused me to take the course I had followed, and when arriving at the battle scene to do everything possible to relieve the condition of the wounded and suffering soldiers." Courtesy of the Lower Cape Fear Historical Society; from the Julian Martin Collection.

Orton House at Orton Plantation Gardens south of Wilmington was built in 1735, with additions in 1840 and 1910. An example of Greek Revival architecture, it is in the center of 10,000 acres of oak trees, azaleas, camellias, water lilies, rhododendron, and palms growing on a bluff above the Cape Fear River. Originally a rice plantation, the estate served as a home and fortress for "King" Roger Moore of the English Lords Proprietors. Orton is the subject of a wall mural in the dining room of Blair House in Washington, D.C., and was the setting for Southern Pines novelist James Boyd's *Marching On*, in which the plantation house is the home of the heroine. The ruin of Provincial Governor Tryon's residence is a half mile distant. Orton Plantation is presently the home of Kenneth M. Sprunt. Courtesy of the Wilmington Chamber of Commerce.

ANTEBELLUM ERA

Wilmington developed a wide reputation for hospitality and generosity in the years between the Revolution and the Civil War. Houses were commodious and well-appointed. Planters with large estates near Wilmington kept houses in town in order to take advantage of social and educational opportunities for their families. By the same token, families with business interests in town built second homes on the nearby sounds so as to escape the summer heat and to participate in water-oriented activities such as sailing and fishing. Airlie Gardens on Wrightsville Sound at Bradley's Creek was created from three such estates, and Orton Plantation south of Wilmington on the Cape Fear River was owned by planters with town connections.

The "Rock Spring" at the foot of Chestnut Street became famous with visitors, who filled their casks with the water which was reputed to have healthful qualities. Commerce thrived. The Bank of Cape Fear, one of the first two banks in North Carolina, was chartered in 1804. The Wilmington and Weldon Railroad, later the Atlantic Coast Line, was founded. The steamer *Step and Fetch-It* ferried travelers across the Cape Fear River. The Wilmington Gas Light Company was organized in 1854, illuminating the town with gas made from lightwood and rosin. A salt works was built near Masonboro Sound. The first building in the state constructed for Masonic Purposes, St. John's Lodge, was erected on Orange Street.

Important visitors came to town. George Washington, John C. Calhoun, James Monroe, Daniel Webster, and the famous "Swedish Nightingale" Jenny Lind were guests of Wilmington. Elegant homes were built by prosperous citizens. The Bellamy Mansion, the deRosset House, the Kenan House, the Latimer House, and the Dudley House lent their lavish facades to the downtown streets. Sections of the town came to be known by such names as Paradise, Sunset Hill, and Dry Pond.

Cultural activities were much in demand. Thalian Hall held its first production in December 1858. Churches, schools, and government offices were built. In 1840, a disastrous fire destroyed 150 buildings along the waterfront, including the Customs House. The Customs House was rebuilt. City Hall, the Marine Hospital, and the Armory of the Wilmington Light Infantry were erected. St. Paul's Lutheran Church, the First Presbyterian Church, St. Thomas Catholic Church, the First Baptist Church, and the Seamen's Bethel came into being. A comfortable way of life with necessary institutions and many pleasures was engineered by Wilmington citizens.

The families of the wealthy were large and required both servants for the houses and laborers for the fields and warehouses. The slave trade was lively. Slaves were bought and sold at the Market House near the Cape Fear River. Runaway slaves and slave uprisings occurred. The turpentine, cotton, and rice industries needed many hands. While some slaves were treated well and often lived in better circumstances than did poor whites, others were not so fortunate. As the first half of the nineteenth century ended, slavery was becoming a national issue which would result in drastic changes in the lifestyle of the people of Wilmington.

Edge Hill was built by Richard Bradley beside Bradley's Creek in 1812 near what is now known as Airlie Gardens. Deeded to the Giles family in 1820 and owned by them until 1839, Edge Hill was surrounded by a white picket fence and had a large barn for the horses and cows which were kept on the estate. Cooking was done by Negro servants in a separate building, with hot food carried to the big house over a boardwalk. A boat house protected the yachts *Pirate* and *Ripple* when they were not in races at the Carolina Yacht Club at Wrightsville Beach. From the Emma Woodward MacMillan Collection; courtesy of James Alfred Miller.

The sailing yacht *Ripple*, number 43, races in the sound near Bradley's Creek. From a private collection.

John Bellamy sits astride a mule at Edge Hill on Bradley Creek around 1900. A lively atmosphere existed on the estate, which had many visitors. An afternoon's crabbing in the waters of Bradley Creek would produce the delicious Edge Hill Crab Cakes for an evening's eating:

Edge Hill Crab Cakes

Mix 1 pound crab meat with 1 slightly beaten egg, 1 teaspoon dry mustard, 2 teaspoons mayonnaise, 1/8 teaspoon pepper, 1 teaspoon Worcestershire sauce, 1 teaspoon Angostura bitters, 1 teaspoon chopped parsley, and 1 teaspoon salt. Make into cakes, dip into milk and cracker crumbs. Place on baking sheet and bake in 375 degree oven for 20 minutes. Serve with Caper sauce.

Photograph from a private collection. Recipe by Mrs. Haskell Rhett, from *Favorite Recipes of the Lower Cape Fear*, published by The Ministering Circle.

In 1925, Robert Drane Jewett and Harriet Bellamy relax in a hammock at Edge Hill on Bradley's Creek shortly before their marriage. From a private collection.

John Bellamy and two ladies of the turn of the century gather beside a boat at Edge Hill on Bradley's Creek during an outing at the sound. In the background is the residence on the Airlie Gardens estate. From a private collection.

Airlie Gardens, owned by the Corbett family, is a 155-acre estate on the Wrightsville Beach road between Bradley Creek and the Inland Waterway at Wrightsville Sound. The grounds are lavishly planted with azaleas, wisteria and giant oak trees hung with Spanish moss. The gardens are composed of a tract of land which originally contained the Richard Bradley estate, the Dr. Adam E. Wright place, and the area known as Sea Side Park. Pembroke Jones acquired the substantial acreage and converted the Sea Side Park Hotel into a many-gabled mansion which contained over thirty bedrooms, a ballroom, and a theater. In this picture taken at Airlie Gardens in 1952, Sue Walton stands beneath the giant Airlie Oak, which is reputed to be over 500 years old. Photograph by Hugh Morton, courtesy of the Greater Wilmington Merchants Association.

The lovely old Lebanon Chapel rests beneath the pines and the Spanish moss at Airlie Gardens. The graveyard nearby contains the graves of many prominent Wilmington citizens, among them members of the Richard Bradley family and the Corbett family. Courtesy of the *Wilmington Star-News.*

The Pembroke Jones mansion at Airlie Gardens, named after an English estate. The mansion was torn down in 1948 and replaced with a modern residence. President of the Cape Fear Rice Milling Company and director of the Carolina Shipbuilding Company, Jones possessed seemingly inexhaustible wealth. The Negroes who lived near his estate celebrated him in song: "I'm gonna live anyhow until I die, die, die/ What folks now are livin' mighty high, high, high/ Now sticks and stones may break mah bones/ But you can't break Mister Pembroke Jones/ I'm gonna live anyhow until I die." Courtesy of the North Carolina Collection, UNC Library, Chapel Hill.

The Smith-Anderson House on the corner of Orange and Front streets is depicted in this early painting which shows the house well-used by its occupants. The Georgian-style structure is the earliest surviving building in Wilmington, built around 1745 by John Smith. Alexander Anderson purchased the house in 1832. The office of Dr. Anderson, located in back of the house, is now relocated on the east side, and the house itself is occupied by Dee Gee's Gift Shop. Courtesy of the Lower Cape Fear Historical Society.

This watercolor of St. John's Lodge on Orange Street was painted by Henry Bacon in 1887. Bacon was the architect for the Lincoln Memorial in Washington D. C., and is buried in Oakdale Cemetery. The architect for the lodge was Joseph Jacobs, a Mason whose descendants live in Wilmington. In 1943, James H. McKoy converted the lodge from its use as a residence for silversmith and jeweler Thomas Brown into a restaurant known as St. John's Tavern. Military personnel stationed in the Wilmington area during World War II frequented the tavern. In 1962, the building became St. John's Art Gallery. Courtesy of the North Carolina State Archives.

The Bank of Cape Fear was incorporated in 1804, with branches in Raleigh, Greensboro, Salem, Asheville, Washington, Salisbury, and Fayetteville. At the southwest corner of Front and Princess streets, the bank was to exist for more than six decades. In the 1840s, its capital was a million and a half dollars. Courtesy of J. Bradford Wiggins.

St. John's Museum of Art, formerly St. John's Art Gallery, was built on Orange Street in 1804 as the home of the oldest Masonic Lodge in North Carolina, St. John's Lodge No. 1, founded in 1755. The museum exhibits from its permanent collection the work of such artists as Miss Elizabeth Chant. Photograph by Joe Nesbitt; courtesy of the *Wilmington Star-News*.

Hinton James was the first student to matriculate at the University of North Carolina at Chapel Hill. After the opening of the university in 1789 as the first state institution to be established in America, James walked from his home in New Hanover County to Chapel Hill, a distance of 150 miles, to secure an education. Around 1828 James, an engineer by profession, worked on the deepening of the channel in the Cape Fear River. His grave is north of Wilmington near Burgaw, in the Hopewell Presbyterian Churchyard. Courtesy of the *Wilmington Star-News*.

The town market house stood at the intersection of Front and Market streets near Market Dock. Here the slave trade was carried on until 1863. Among the slaves in the Wilmington area was Peter, who was set free in 1751 by Sarah Allen with the use of four acres, suits of winter and summer clothes, and four bushels of Indian corn. In 1790, Francis Clayton freed his slave Brunetta, and in 1803, Magdalin Mary Toomer freed her female slave Tamar Moran. Tony was a slave owned by Mrs. Eliza Bradley in 1838, and he lived in a residence between Red Cross and Walnut streets and Second and Third streets, with a number of other slaves living nearby.

Despite the slavery associated with the market house, black writer Jack Thorne grew up in Wilmington with fond memories of the market bell. Early in the 1900s, in *Tender Recollections of Wilmington, N.C.*, he wrote in a poem called "The Old Market Bell of Wilmington":

I can hear its peals to-day
Altho' years have passed away,
Since, like some Minstrel's
  lay
Its merry chime,
Heralded the crimson dawn,
Of each succeeding morn
In notes sublime. . . .

In that dear old home again
  I dwell
Whenever I think of the
  Market Bell.

Courtesy of the New Hanover County Museum.

This sketch of Bradley's Wharf was made in May 1837 by a traveler on a boat from New York to New Zealand. Drawn from the boat's anchorage in the Cape Fear River at Wilmington, the view depicts a wharf, thought to belong to merchant Richard Bradley, and streets and houses of the town. Gift of Gladys McGill; courtesy of the New Hanover County Museum.

Jack Thorne, pictured here, was actually Wilmington's David Bryant Fulton. Thorne's *Hanover* is a personal narrative of the 1898 Race Riots in Wilmington. The author's feelings about his hometown were both loving and critical. His words from *Tender Recollections of Wilmington, N.C.*, "Wilmington, Oh My Beloved! The incendiary cry of the agitator and traducer of yesterday which amazed the world and tarnished thy good name could not hush the song of birds..." bring to mind an earlier black revolutionary writer David Walker, who was born in Wilmington in 1785 as the son of a slave and a free woman.

In 1866, David Elias Sadgwar, with (left to right) Alfred Hargrave, Henry Taylor, and James Cutlar, founded Chestnut Street United Presbyterian Church. Courtesy of Felice Sadgwar.

24

David Elias Sadgwar was born in Wilmington in 1811 to a visiting French sea captain and the daughter of a prominent white family. According to the Sadgwar family memoirs, the sea captain had departed Wilmington before his son's birth, and the illegitimate white baby was given to a black slave mammy to wetnurse and rear as her own child. Growing up among slaves, the white child was legally a slave and a member of the Negro race.

A carpenter and cabinetmaker, Sadgwar married a blue-eyed black slave named Fanny Merrick, by whom he had seven children. The first two children were fair-skinned, with straight hair and blue eyes. Not content with slavery, Sadgwar dressed his wife as a mammy and ran away from North Carolina with his family. In New York State, the group was spotted as runaways and returned to Wilmington to be incarcerated behind the Bellamy Mansion at the corner of Fifth and Market streets. Because of crowding and lack of sanitation, the two babies contracted scarlet fever, typhoid fever, and dysentery, and died.

When Abraham Lincoln freed the slaves, Sadgwar was provided with a plantation on the Castle Hayne Road and came into ownership of large portions of the block of Fifth and Brunswick streets. His sons, Frederick and Daniel, were taught carpentry and cabinetmaking, and their pieces are owned by Wilmington families today.

The history of the Sadgwar family is not unique, but is representative of many black families. Even during the days of slavery, the children of slaves were sent to school and exposed to cultural activities. Church schools were opened all over the South after the Civil War by such groups as the Missionary Society of the Congregational Church, utilizing teachers who had graduated from Wellesley, Sarah Lawrence, Mt. Holyoke, Yale and Harvard. The high level of education and culture and the mixed blood of the Sadgwar family are characteristic of other Wilmington black families. Courtesy of Felice Sadgwar.

Frederick Cutlar Sadgwar was born in 1843 to David Elias Sadgwar and Fanny Merrick. He was the father of Felice and Mabel Sadgwar and ten other children. Courtesy of Felice Sadgwar.

Fanny Merrick, right, was the wife of David Elias Sadgwar. She is pictured here with her sister Adealede. Courtesy of Felice Sadgwar.

Daniel Sadgwar was the brother of Sophie and Fanny Sadgwar. Courtesy of Felice Sadgwar.

Sophie Sadgwar (left) and Fanny Sadgwar (center) with friend Blon Richardson. The Sadgwar sisters were the daughters of David Elias Sadgwar. Courtesy of Felice Sadgwar.

The Sadgwar family, prominent members of the black community in Wilmington, gather on the steps of their primary residence at 15 North Eighth Street after the funeral of Frederick C. Sadgwar in 1925. Felice Sadgwar, far right, was the youngest of twelve Sadgwar children and became a teacher of music in the Wilmington public schools. Mabel Sadgwar, second from left in the second row, became a beautician known for her elegant style of dress. Their mother, Caroline Sadgwar, third row center, was Cherokee Indian. Courtesy of Felice Sadgwar.

Carrie Sadgwar, daughter of Frederick Sadgwar, married Wilmington newspaper publisher Alex Manly, whose *Daily Record* offices were burned in the 1898 Wilmington Race Riots. She is shown here with her son Milo, whose brother was Lewin. When Carrie Sadgwar attended Gregory Normal Institute, her teachers discovered her excellent singing voice. Subsequently, she became the lead soprano in Fisk University's Mozart Society and a member of the Fisk Jubilee Singers who performed at Covent Garden for Queen Victoria. The *Irish Times* reported that "one of the most pleasing selections of the evening was 'Old Folks At Home' which was sung by Miss Carrie Sadgwar." Courtesy of Felice Sadgwar.

This document signed by S. S. Ashley, Superintendent of Education in Wilmington, gives Frederick C. Sadgwar permission in 1868 to establish a School for Freedmen at Whiteville. It was approved by Allan Rutherford, Captain of the Forty-Fourth U. S. Infantry. Courtesy of Felice Sadgwar.

The Zebulon Latimer House on South Third Street as it appears today. Restored by the Lower Cape Fear Historical Society, the house serves as its headquarters. In 1852, Wilmington merchant Zebulon Latimer built the antebellum residence for his family. The Latimer family helped found the Wilmington Seacoast Railroad in 1888. Listed in the National Register of Historic Places, the Latimer House is open to the public. Courtesy of the Greater Wilmington Chamber of Commerce.

The servant's quarters behind the Zebulon Latimer House on South Third Street have been restored by the Lower Cape Fear Historical Society. Slaves were an important part of the life of early Wilmington, working in the cotton industry, the turpentine industry, and as domestics. Slavery was introduced into North Carolina by Colonial Governor John Yeamans from Barbados in 1671. In 1742 the population of New Hanover County was 3,000, including 2,000 Negroes. In 1831 a Negro uprising resulted in four hangings of slaves on Princess Street and the shootings of several other slaves whose heads were placed on poles in conspicuous places to serve as warnings to members of the Negro race. From the Julian Martin Collection; courtesy of the Lower Cape Fear Historical Society.

Zebulon Latimer was a partner in the W. & Z. Latimer dry goods business in Wilmington and the Bank of Cape Fear. Married to Elizabeth Savage, the oldest native-born citizen of Wilmington and the oldest member of St. James Episcopal Church at the time of her death in 1904, Zebulon Latimer is buried in Oakdale Cemetery along with his wife. From the Pickrell Collection; courtesy of the Lower Cape Fear Historical Society.

The grandsons of Zebulon Latimer, Herbert Latimer (left) and Empie Latimer (right) were the sons of Fannie Empie and Herbert Latimer. From the Pickrell Collection; courtesy of the Lower Cape Fear Historical Society.

ARMORY OF THE WILMINGTON LIGHT INFANTRY

The Armory of the Wilmington Light Infantry on Market Street was the site of the new Hanover County Public Library until March 1981, when the library moved into new quarters at the site of Belk-Beery department store downtown. The Wilmington Light Infantry was organized in 1853 as an active military unit. In 1886, WLI was in charge of Wilmington under martial law established after the disastrous waterfront fire which destroyed many stores and residences, at a loss of one million dollars. During World War I, members of the WLI in France were in Battery C, Second Battalion, Trench Artillery. The WLI has been called out for periods of crisis and has served as an honor guard at many official celebrations. Photograph by C. W. Yates and Company; courtesy of the North Carolina Collection, UNC Library, Chapel Hill.

This view of the Atlantic Coast Line Railroad yards and depot shows its relation to the Cape Fear River at the northern tip of Wilmington. First called the Wilmington and Raleigh Railroad Company and then the Wilmington and Weldon Railroad, it was the longest railroad in the world when the 162 miles of track were completed in 1840. Courtesy of the North Carolina Collection, UNC Library, Chapel Hill.

The Governor Dudley mansion on South Front Street is the headquarters of the Historic Wilmington Foundation directed by R. V. Asbury. Built in 1825, the house was the residence of Governor Edward B. Dudley, who was the first governor elected by the people of North Carolina. The first railroad in the state, the Wilmington and Weldon Railroad, was founded in 1835 by prominent Wilmington citizens who met in Dudley's bedchamber. Dudley became president of the railroad line.

During the 1890s, Pembroke Jones owned the house high above the banks of the Cape Fear River. When fire damaged the residence, Jones moved his family to Airlie Gardens on Wrightsville Sound, and James Sprunt became the owner of the Dudley mansion. The major historian of the area known as Cape Fear, Sprunt reared his family in the house. In 1909, the Sprunts entertained President Taft during his visit to Wilmington. Other visitors have been Daniel Webster, James Cardinal Gibbons, and William Tecumseh Sherman. Courtesy of the Greater Wilmington Chamber of Commerce.

The legend of the Maco Light was born in 1868, when Joe Baldwin, a conductor for the Wilmington and Weldon Railroad Line, was killed with a lantern in his hand as he stood on the tracks at Maco station fourteen miles northwest of Wilmington. Decapitated in the accident, Joe Baldwin is said to be in search of his head, swinging his lantern as he moves down the tracks. The ghostly light appeared for the first time shortly after Baldwin's death and has been investigated numerous times. Yet to be attributed to natural causes, the light shows itself on dewy, moonless nights following warm days, and has become an attraction for Wilmington courting couples. Photograph of Maco Light reenactment by Don Davis, Jr.; courtesy of the *Wilmington Star-News*.

This playbill announces the first production of the Thalian Association in the new Thalian Hall on December 3, 1858. *The Invisible Prince, or The Island of Tranquil Delights* was performed in an auditorium which held 950 people and was lighted by 188 gas burners. The Thalian Association is the oldest little theater group in America and was founded in 1788. Members have included Dr. Adam Empie, rector of St. James Parish; the Reverend R. B. Drane; and Dr. Thomas Wright. Courtesy of Thalian Hall.

THALIAN HALL!

THE MEMBERS OF THE THALIAN ASSOCIATION

WILL GIVE THEIR

First Representation!

IN THEIR

NEW HALL!

On Friday Ev'ng, Dec. 3d,

When they will perform the

Invisible Prince,

OR

THE ISLAND OF TRANQUIL DELIGHTS.

This late 1800s view of Thalian Hall shows its relation to City Hall. Thalian Hall, on the right side of the building, is in the east wing of City Hall. James F. Post served as superintendent of construction of the combined government offices and theater built on the site of Innes Academy at the corner of Third and Princess streets. In 1902, the theater was called The Academy of Music and was also known as the Opera House. In 1964, the Junior League of Wilmington helped establish a commission to renovate and restore Thalian Hall. Tyrone Power, who visited Wilmington in 1958, stated that Thalian Hall was "one of the three great theaters in the world," citing it with the Drottningholm Royal Palace near Stockholm and the Theater Royal in Bristol, England. Courtesy of Thalian Hall.

This detail of the proscenium of Thalian Hall shows fluted Corinthian columns and intricate rococo design. Overhead were gold ceiling rosettes. Mural-like paintings decorated the side walls. The lower balcony was trimmed in Italian green leather upholstery. In the stage floor, trap doors opened into the basement, permitting actors or stage set to disappear. In 1864, tickets to a production at Thalian Hall were not cheap, reflecting the inflation of the war. Admission was $5. Courtesy of Thalian Hall.

The cornerstone of City Hall was laid on December 27, 1855, with St. John's Lodge No. 1 in charge of the ceremonies. Lodge Master Isaac Northrop presided, and a procession marched to the corner of Princess and Third streets from the Masonic Hall. Papers deposited in the cornerstone included the names of town and county officials, names of the registered voters in Wilmington, and the address of Thomas Loring, editor of the *Commercial* newspaper. The City Hall was built jointly with Thalian Hall, which has its entrance at the right side of the building on Princess Street. Courtesy of the North Carolina Collection, UNC Library, Chapel Hill.

Demolished in 1915, this is the second U. S. Customs House in Wilmington. The first Customs House was destroyed by the Wilmington waterfront fire of 1840, which razed more than 150 buildings. Courtesy of the North Carolina State Archives.

The Marine Hospital at the corner of Eighth and Nun streets was distinguished by an octagonal cupola. Built in 1857 for the purpose of treating sick seamen, this Marine Hospital succeeded the first Marine Hospital three miles south of Wilmington administered by Dr. A. J. deRossett. The Marine Hospital pictured here no longer stands. Courtesy of the North Carolina Collection, UNC Library, Chapel Hill.

St. Thomas Catholic Church was established in 1845, with the Reverend Thomas Murphy the priest in charge. In 1868, Cardinal Gibbons wrote his famous work. *The Faith of Our Fathers*, while vicar here. This picture of the church was made in 1966 just after a fire in the church's interior. The church is now a performing arts center.
Photograph by Herbert Howard.

Elizabeth Bridgers and Emma Bellamy Williamson Hendren are costumed as theatergoers of the 1800s as they ride in a horse-drawn carriage in front of Thalian Hall. Elizabeth Bridgers organized scrapbooks depicting the history of Thalian Hall and was a member of the Bridgers family who lived in the Bridgers House on South Third Street. R. R. Bridgers was president of the Atlantic Coast Line Railroad. Emma Bellamy Williamson Hendren is a member of the Bellamy family whose home stands at the corner of Fifth and Market streets and is known as the Bellamy Mansion.
Courtesy of Thalian Hall.

The Bellamy mansion at the corner of Fifth and Market streets was built by Dr. John D. Bellamy in 1857 as his family residence. The ornate, five-story structure was the Federal military headquarters during the occupation of Wilmington in the Civil War and was occupied by General Joseph R. Hawley. Opened to the public in recent years, the house suffered a fire which did severe damage to the interior's elegant furnishings. Courtesy of the *Wilmington Star-News*.

CIVIL WAR ERA

After President Lincoln was elected in November 1860, the citizens of Wilmington made the approaching struggle with the North their major topic of conversation. Attorney George Davis became known for his eloquence on the subject, later being appointed Attorney General of the Confederacy. Secession rallies and flag-raisings were held. The telegraph service brought news of growing insurrection. The Lone Star state flag of North Carolina was hoisted by Wilmington secessionists in 1861 before the state became the last to formally secede from the Union. Soon the Stars and Bars battleflag of the Confederacy was flying.

In January 1861, the Cape Fear Minute Men and the Committee of Safety took possession of Fort Johnston and Fort Caswell. Later, the forts were taken again by the Wilmington Light Infantry, the German Volunteers, and the Wilmington Rifle Guards. The Federal Blockade of the Cape Fear River led to the construction of the largest earthwork of the Civil War, Fort Fisher. Wilmington's excellent railroads made it a dispersing point for Confederate troops and a rest area for the wounded. Blockade-running became the town's most important function, and the streets were filled with agents conducting Confederate business with European governments.

In 1862, a devastating yellow fever epidemic caused over 500 deaths in Wilmington. The citizens fled by private carriage and railroad car to distant places or took refuge at the sounds. The night air was considered deadly, for the real cause of the disease was yet to be discovered. Many prominent citizens lost their lives during the plague. Oakdale cemetery filled with bodies of the dead. In November, a killing frost ended the October slaughter.

The war and the blockade-running continued. On the night of January 12, 1865, the Federal fleet assembled off Fort Fisher "the most formidable armada the world has ever known" and opened fire the next morning in a two-day bombardment. On January 15, the Federal troops engaged in hand-to-hand combat with Confederate forces. After seven hours, the Confederates surrendered. Wilmington was occupied on February 22, and the fighting ended in the Cape Fear region.

The residences of the town were tightly closed and blinds were drawn. General Joseph R. Hawley occupied the house of Dr. John Bellamy at Fifth and Market streets. The rector of St. James Church, Dr. A. A. Watson, refused to offer prayers for the President of the United States and was forced to surrender the keys of the church to General Hawley. The pews were thrown into the street, and the building was converted into a military hospital. An oath of allegiance was required of all businessmen in Wilmington who wished to continue in operation.

The new status of the Negro freed servants from masters. Some slaves seized the opportunity to walk away, while others elected to stay in the homes which were familiar to them. When the Confederate army surrendered at Appomattox in April 1865, the soldiers from Wilmington slowly returned to their families and their private lives. A large number of officers had been killed in service, among them Colonel Gaston Meares, Colonel William M. Parsley, and Captain J. A. Wright. A graveyard was created in 1867 on Market Street for the bodies of the Union soldiers killed in battle, and a monument to the Confederate dead was erected in Oakdale Cemetery in 1872.

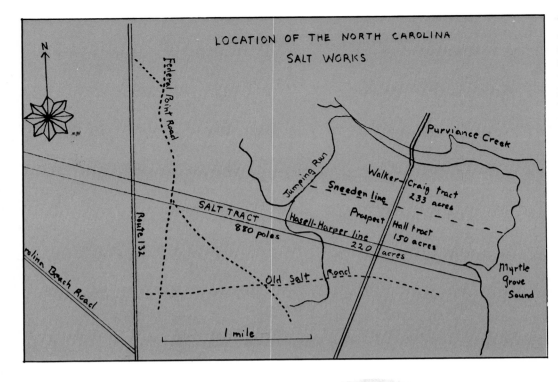

LOCATION OF THE NORTH CAROLINA
SALT WORKS

N

Federal Point Road

Route 132

Carolina Beach Road

Purviance Creek

Jumping Run

Walker-Craig tract
233 acres

Sneeden line

Prospect Hall tract
150 acres

SALT TRACT
880 poles

Hasell-Harper line
220 acres

Old Salt Road

Myrtle Grove Sound

1 mile

This map shows the location of the North Carolina State Salt Works at Myrtle Grove Sound. On the site conveyed to the state by Oscar Grant Parsley in 1862, the salt works in 1864 produced 62,000 bushels of the vital ingredient. From *Salt—That Necessary Article*, by Isabel H. Williams and Leora H. McEachern.

Judah P. Benjamin lived in Wilmington in his early youth and became a prominent Jewish lawyer and statesman. Benjamin held three positions in the cabinet of the Confederate States of America: attorney-general, secretary of state, and secretary of war. Gift of Ida B. Kellam; courtesy of the Lower Cape Fear Historical Society.

These two views from *Harper's Pictorial History of the Civil War,* October 1864, show the Confederate blockading fleet off Wilmington at New Inlet and Old Inlet, in sun and rain. The Wilmington Light Infantry occupied a large and commanding battery on Federal Point at New Inlet which had been built in 1861 by Captain Charles P. Bolles and was called Battery Bolles. This was the beginning of Fort Fisher, named in honor of Colonel Charles F. Fisher, who had been killed in the first battle of Manassas.

Fort Fisher was an extensive fortification stretching along the ocean and to the Cape Fear River. Colonel William Lamb was placed in charge of construction of the Fort Fisher parapets in 1862. His wife, Daisy Chaffee Lamb, was called the "Angel of Fort Fisher" for her service to sick and wounded Confederate soldiers. Living in a lonely hut north of Fort Fisher with only pine knots for light and heat, under constant exposure to shot and shell during the bombardment, the brave woman remained near her husband until the end of the war, despite the death of an infant son. When Confederate spy Rose Greenhow drowned off Fort Fisher in September 1864, Mrs. Lamb helped prepare the body for burial in Wilmington. Parted from Colonel Lamb after the fall of Fort Fisher, Daisy Lamb eventually located him in a Federal hospital and subsequently bore a family of eleven children. Courtesy of the North Carolina State Archives.

Fort Fisher below Wilmington near Southport. Courtesy of the *Wilmington Star-News.*

A view of Fort Fisher from a Mound Battery during attack. The Confederate flag flies above the cannon. Courtesy of the *Wilmington Star-News.*

This Armstrong gun battery was part of the sea defense at Fort Fisher. The photograph was taken around 1865. Courtesy of the North Carolina State Archives.

Rose O'Neill Greenhow, Confederate spy, at the Old Capitol prison in Washington, D. C., with her eight-year-old daughter, Rose, in 1862. Mrs. Greenhow lost her life in service to the Southern cause. After being released from the prison, she was attempting to bear special dispatches to Wilmington from Europe when her transport, the steamer *Condor*, ran aground off Fort Fisher. Mrs. Greenhow drowned in the breakers. Her body was found on the beach and brought to Wilmington to be laid in state at the Seaman's Bethel. In a funeral conducted with full military honors, the body of Mrs. Greenhow was wrapped in the Confederate flag and interred at Oakdale Cemetery with a monument commemorating her bravery. On May 10 of each year, the Daughters of the Confederacy decorate the grave of Rose Greenhow with a small Confederate flag as they place flags on all the graves of the Confederate soldiers. Photograph by Mathew Brady; courtesy of the New Hanover County Museum.

43

The United Daughters of the Confederacy decorate the grave of Confederate spy Rose Greenhow in Oakdale Cemetery as members of the Wilmington Light Infantry stand by. This picture of the annual event was made during the early 1930s. Courtesy of the New Hanover County Public Library.

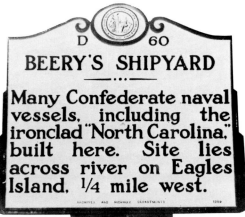

D 60

BEERY'S SHIPYARD

Many Confederate naval vessels, including the ironclad "North Carolina," built here. Site lies across river on Eagles Island, 1/4 mile west.

During the Civil War, two large shipyards in Wilmington built and repaired ships. Beery's Shipyard was located across from the city on the Cape Fear River at Eagles Island. The ironclad *North Carolina* was constructed here in 1862. An attempt was also made at this shipyard to build a submarine, but the boat was never put into service. In 1864, the ironclad *Raleigh* was built at Cassidy's Shipyard at the foot of Church Street. The *Raleigh* was commanded by Captain Pembroke Jones. Courtesy of the *Wilmington Star-News*.

The Confederate blockade-runner *Colonel Lamb* was built in Liverpool, England. Courtesy of the *Wrightsville Beach Gazette*.

Captain John Newland Maffitt, a commander in the Confederate Navy, was a native of Wilmington who left for the sea when he was thirteen years old. Resigning his commission in the U. S. Navy in 1861, he took charge of the blockade-runner *Florida* until 1864, and subsequently commanded the blockade runners *Owl* and *Lilian*. The Cape Fear River tourboat *Captain J. N. Maffitt*, named after the famous Confederate naval officer, cruises daily from Chandler's Wharf. Photograph by S. W. Gault; gift of Sidney Briggs; from the Julian Martin Collection; courtesy of the Lower Cape Fear Historical Society.

James Sprunt as a young man when he was purser aboard the blockade runner *Lilian*. Sprunt later became a well-known Wilmington historian whose volumes have been indispensable in charting the events of the Cape Fear area. Courtesy of the New Hanover County Public Library.

Harbor of Wilmington
N. C.

Opposite Page:
The Wilmington harbor is pictured on the board of a Blockade Runner game marketed during the nineteenth century and derived from the Civil War enterprise. During the period from May 1863 to December 1864, 260 blockade-running vessels came into Wilmington carrying cargoes of sugar, cloth, liquor, candles, and "Nassau bacon" and left with exports of Confederate cotton and naval stores. Agents and traders involved in blockade-running converged on Wilmington, creating great commercial activity. The many Englishmen in town dressed extravagantly and occupied a large yellow house on Market Street where they fought cocks on Sundays and entertained lavishly. Blockade-running, for all its dangers, offered excitement and handsome profits for its participants. Courtesy of the North Carolina State Archives.

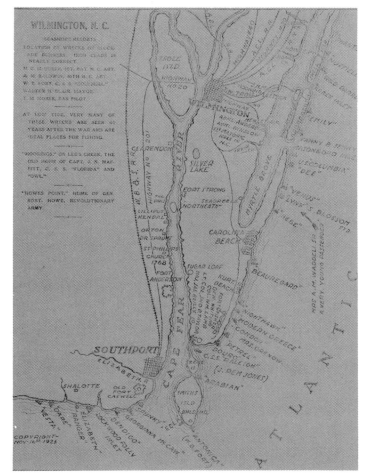

This map shows the location of blockade-runners wrecked near Wilmington. At low tide, many of these shipwrecks may be seen. Along Wrightsville Beach are the *Fanny and Jenny*, the *Wild Darrell*, the *Phantom*, the *Emily*, and the *Nutfield*. Near Carolina Beach are the *Venus*, the *Lynx*, the *Hebe*, and the *Beauregard*. Off Kure Beach and along Fort Fisher are the *Nighthawk*, the *Modern Greece*, the *Condor*, the *Petrel*, and the *Raleigh*. The *Arabian* and the *Antonica* lie off Baldhead Island. Near Fort Caswell are the *Spunky*, the *Georgiana McCaw*, and the *Bendigo*. At Shallotte are the *Elizabeth*, the *Ranger*, the *Dare*, and the *Vesta*. The map was prepared in 1925 by Captain R. N. Sweet. Courtesy of the North Carolina State Archives.

On December 27, 1852, a charter was granted for a new cemetery to be constructed on a neck of land on Burnt Mill Creek. The cemetery was named Oakdale and still exists as a place of winding drives and moss-hung oaks. Wilmington families continue to be buried in the beautiful plots, the first burial being that of the young daughter of Dr. A. J. deRosset in 1855. The Negro cemetery, Pine Forest, is nearby. This picture of Oakdale Cemetery was made in April 1907. Courtesy of the North Carolina State Archives.

This tombstone is in Oakdale Cemetery beneath the Spanish moss. The old cemetery has a number of unusual graves, including that of Nancy Adams Martin, who was buried seated in a chair in a large cask of alcohol. The young woman was the daughter of a sea captain named Silas Martin, who made his home in Wilmington. She died while aboard ship, and her body was preserved in liquor so that it could be brought home for a Christian burial. Photograph by Knickerbocker; courtesy of the *Wilmington Star-News.*

Reverend Robert B. Drane, D. D., was rector of St. James Episcopal Church during the Wilmington yellow fever epidemic of 1862. Reverend Drane contracted the disease as he ministered to the sick and gave up his own life.

Prior to his death, Reverend Drane gave to St. James Church the marble baptismal font from which he and succeeding ministers christened the new life of the congregation. Courtesy of St. James Episcopal Church.

Emilie Beauregard Bailey was born in 1861 and died in 1862, in the same year that a yellow fever epidemic killed many other Wilmington citizens. The disease was brought to the city in the hold of a blockade runner which tied up at a dock in the Cape Fear River. Within weeks after two sailors from the vessel died while the ship was in port, many people experienced the yellow fever plague. Nearly 300 bodies were buried in a mass burial at Oakdale Cemetery as a result of the illness. In all, 448 citizens died. At the height of the epidemic, those who could flee did, jamming the roads out of the city. Death carts carried bodies to the cemetery, and burning tar barrels were set out by physicians to purify the air. By Christmas, a frost had come and the plague was gone, but not before it had claimed the lives of Dr. James H. Dickson, Reverend Robert Drane of St. James Episcopal Church, Reverend John L. Pritchard of the First Baptist Church, and Reverend Father Thomas Murphy of St. Thomas Roman Catholic Church. Courtesy of the New Hanover County Museum.

48

The monument to the Confederate dead was dedicated in Oakdale Cemetery in 1872, two years after the first Confederate Memorial Day was observed in Wilmington. Courtesy of the New Hanover County Public Library.

The figure atop the Confederate Memorial looks over surrounding Oakdale Cemetery. Photograph by John Sears; courtesy of the *Wilmington Star-News*.

This view of Wilmington during the Civil War was drawn by a newspaper artist on February 27, 1865, just after the city was occupied by Federal troops. Released Yankee prisoners file down South Front Street and turn the corner at Dock Street to reach ships which will take them home. Included in the drawing are the Federal fleet, the Customs House, and the Town Hall. Courtesy of the *Wilmington Star-News*.

Attending this Confederate Veterans' meeting in 1910 are Dr. William Baldwin, Reverend Andrew J. Howell, Edgar Williams, Henry Kuhl, Richard Reaves, Dr. William Dougald MacMillan, and Benjamin Franklin Hall. During reunions, the Civil War veterans would camp in tents erected on Market Street between Water and Second streets and visit in' homes of Wilmington citizens. The town would be gaily decorated with Confederate flags, and many festivities would be held. From the Jennewein Collection; courtesy of the Lower Cape Fear Historical Society.

The National Cemetery's quiet rows of white markers are reminders of the war dead buried in this serene graveyard on Market Street at Burnt Mill Creek. Nearby is Chestnut Street Elementary School, and in the mornings and afternoons young children walk along the wall beneath the trees which shade those who died in service to their country. Courtesy of the New Hanover County Public Library

A number rather than a name marks the grave of an unknown soldier who rests in Wilmington National Cemetery beneath the sheltering trees. Number 1811 is among thousands of Union soldiers who gave up their lives during the Civil War and lie in the peaceful graveyard created in 1867. Courtesy of the *Wilmington Star-News.*

This monument to the Confederate soldiers stands at the intersection of Third and Dock streets, provided from a bequest of G.J. Boney, Confederate soldier. Courtesy of the North Carolina Collection, UNC Library, Chapel Hill.

Young boys and girls enjoy an afternoon of boating on Burnt Mill Creek near the National Cemetery. This picture was made around 1930. Courtesy of the New Hanover County Public Library.

Boating on the Cape Fear River in the late 1800s. In the background, the city of Wilmington can be seen with the spires of churches and masts of sailing ships rising above the trees. Courtesy of the New Hanover County Museum.

RECONSTRUCTION

On February 20, 1866, Wilmington again became a city by charter from the North Carolina General Assembly. A. H. Van Bokkelen was selected mayor, with a Board of Aldermen which included O. G. Parsley, James G. Burr, A. E. Hall, and W. A. Wright. Former Confederate General Robert Ransom was Marshal of Police. The Wilmington Chamber of Commerce was organized, and the Cape Fear Club was established as a gathering place for Wilmington gentlemen.

The following year, the *Wilmington Morning Star* issued its first edition. A system of horse-drawn cars was created by the Sea Side Railroad Company with a line down Market Street to Front Street to the terminal of the Atlantic Coast Line Railroad, then called the Wilmington and Weldon Railroad. Business was brisk.

River improvements were made with funds appropriated by Congress. A great engineering project under the direction of Captain Francis Bacon was begun to close New Inlet. The improved riverway boosted many businesses, among them the turpentine, lumber, cotton, fertilizer, and general shipping industries. Wilmington became a major industrial port.

The future President of the United States, Woodrow Wilson, came to stay in Wilmington in 1874 at the Presbyterian manse at Fourth and Orange streets, where his father was minister. The bustling activity of the port city fascinated the sickly young man, who was recuperating from chronic illness. The steamers made excursions on the Cape Fear River to Southport; the schooners docked at the wharves on Water Street. The extraordinary Shell Road from Wilmington to Wrightsville was completed in 1876, and the Wilmington Sea Coast Railway to Hammocks (now Harbor Island) was soon constructed.

Downtown businesses were established, with stores of all kinds appearing. In 1880, clothing merchant S. H. Fishblate was elected mayor. Churches and schools proliferated. The Temple of Israel was built at Fourth and Market streets by members of the Jewish community. The Cape Fear Military Academy established by General R. E. Colston came under the direction of Professor Washington Catlett, giving up its military aspect. Amy Bradley came to Wilmington from New England to establish a public school with funds provided by Mary Tileston Hemenway. The Young Men's Christian Association organized money-raising events for a building.

The first telephone was installed in Wilmington in 1878. The first electric lights were operated in 1886. In that same year, a disastrous fire destroyed a large part of the waterfront, and the Charleston earthquake caused walls and chimneys to topple as far north as Wilmington. To round off the eventful year, a great blizzard occurred.

In the 1890s, the political picture became confused. An evolution in state politics brought a Republican-Fusion city government to Wilmington. Negroes held public office and began to assert their power. Feeling in black and white communities became polarized, and the tensions erupted on November 10, 1898, two days after election day. Resolutions by former Congressman Alfred Waddell condemned a Negro-owned newspaper, the *Record,* for its editorials on racial matters. The resolutions also demanded the resignation of the mayor, chief of police and Board of Aldermen and stated that citizens of New Hanover County would not be ruled by men of African origin.

Armed white citizens gathered at the Armory of the Wilmington Light Infantry and made a procession out Market Street to Seventh Street to the offices of the *Record.* Printing equipment was destroyed and the building set ablaze. Later, a group of Negroes was attacked with Winchester rifles and pistols, resulting in several deaths. The Negroes in the city became terrified, many of them fleeing to nearby Navassa. The military restored order in Wilmington, and Colonel Waddell was installed as mayor.

On February 10, 1899, a snowstorm began which covered the streets of the city with a foot of snow. On November 1, a violent hurricane struck the area and destroyed many cottages and other buildings at Wrightsville Beach. The massive trestle of the Sea Coast Railroad was twisted from its moorings, and the lovely Shell Road was a mass of debris. The period of reconstruction after the Civil War ended in turmoil with race riots and natural disasters. The nineteenth century went out with a bang and ushered in a more stable era.

This drawing depicts smugglers at Masonboro Sound. In 1867, *Harper's Weekly* described an attack by U.S. revenue officers at this location, saying, "The smugglers were foreigners, speaking broken English." The smugglers' boat capsized and sent to the bottom the three sailors and their boxes of goods.

The same incident appeared in the *Wilmington Daily Journal* on November 5, 1867. "It was subsequently determined that the boat was engaged in smuggling cigars," commented the newspaper article. The smuggling took place at Purviance Creek, which came to be named Whiskey Creek in the 1860s. Legend has it that whiskey was smuggled both in and out of the area. An eyewitness to the violence and trafficking which occurred here was the wife of Dr. Edwin Anderson, who was walking on the terrace outside her home one night when she saw one Portuguese sailor kill another beside her home. Courtesy of the North Carolina Collection, UNC Library, Chapel Hill.

This view from across the
Cape Fear River shows
Wilmington as it appeared
in the late 1800s, the old
Customs House at center,
and Water Street between
Market and Princess streets.
Courtesy of the North
Carolina State Archives.

THE MORNING STAR.

The first front page of the
Wilmington Morning Star,
printed on October 15, 1867.
In this issue, owner William
H. Bernard set forth the
purpose and responsibilities
of the newspaper. The price
of the paper was three cents.
Courtesy of the *Wilmington
Star-News*.

The *Wilmington Star-News* offices were on Chestnut Street in 1930, shown here behind the State Champions and their band. The Friendly Cafeteria and the Cape Fear Hotel shared the block with the *Star-News*. Established in 1867 by Major William H. Bernard, the *Morning Star* was conservative in its policies and was aligned with the Democrats. The newspaper is presently located on South Seventeenth Street. Courtesy of the New Hanover County Public Library.

The Cape Fear Club in this picture stood at Front and Chestnut streets and was established in 1866 as the oldest men's club in North Carolina. Incorporated to promote "literary and social intercourse," it was surrounded by trees and had a wide piazza. In 1912, the club built new quarters on the corner of Second and Chestnut streets. Photograph by C. W. Yates and Company; courtesy of the North Carolina Collection, UNC Library, Chapel Hill.

Wilmington business and professional men enjoy one of the social events of the Cape Fear Club, a shrimp and beer party in the summer of 1965.

For many years, the famous "Cape Fear Club Punch" has been served by Wilmingtonians at festive occasions:

Cape Fear Club Punch

Mix 4 quarts straight Bourbon or Rye, 1 quart Jamaica Rum, 1 pint Cognac, 1½ quarts green tea, 1½ pints strained lemon juice, and 6 tablespoons sugar. Set aside in an airtight vessel for several weeks (may be kept for years). Using ½ gallon stock, 2 quarts sparkling water, and 2 quarts champagne, serve in punchbowl over ice, garnished with 2 sliced oranges and 2 sliced lemons.

Photograph from *The Cape Fear Club*, by Al G. Dickson. Recipe from the Leila James Wootten Collection.

This program is from the early years of the L'Arioso Club, which was established in 1871 as the L'Allegro Soiree Club, soon called the L'Arioso Pleasure Club. In 1881, the name was changed to the L'Arioso German Club. The social organization put on dances, utilizing ballrooms in such buildings as the Masonic Temple and the Cape Fear Country Club. Mrs. John D. Bellamy was an active member of L'Arioso, as were Pembroke Jones, H. B. Jewett, and George N. Harriss. Gift of Lucile Murchison Marvin; courtesy of the William Madison Randall Library at the University of North Carolina at Wilmington.

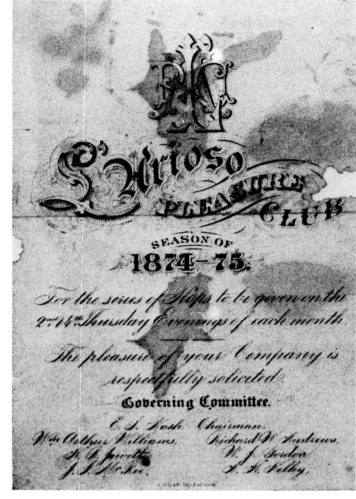

The Bollman Truss Bridge was built in 1868 over the northeast branch of the Cape Fear River for the Wilmington Railway Bridge Company. Two miles of timber trestling connected the structure with a companion bridge over the northwest branch of the river. Here Wendel Bollman poses with colleagues upon completion of the span. Bollman was a pioneer in structural engineering patenting the Bollman system of diagonally trussed links with a cast-iron compression chord in 1852 and designing the four spans at Harper's Ferry in 1862. A self-taught civil engineer from Baltimore, Bollman achieved what has been called the "greatest single step in the history of civil engineering" with the use of iron as a primary structural material. He sits second from the right with his cane leaning against his knee. Photograph by Van Orsdell; courtesy of the North Carolina State Archives.

The Old Wilmington Depot
was the last stop on the line
for the Atlantic Coast Line
Railroad, the terminus. The
trains would cross the
trestle on the Cape Fear
River and move into the
station at the northern tip
of the city, where they would
discharge and take on
passengers. John, one of the
porters at the station, would
help the passengers with
their luggage and often take
them to the Orton Hotel on
Front Street for lodging.
Courtesy of the North
Carolina Collection, UNC
Library, Chapel Hill.

The U. S. Post Office was built in 1888 at a cost of $100,000 on the site of the former home of R. R. Bridgers at the corner of Front and Chestnut streets. Made of granite from Wadesboro, North Carolina, the building had two faces carved over the entrance, one happy, the other dejected. It was said that one face had received a letter, the other had received none. The handsome edifice was demolished when the present Post Office was built. Across the street was the Cape Fear Club. The first Wilmington Postmaster was John Bradley. Photograph by C. W. Yates and Company; courtesy of the North Carolina Collection, UNC Library, Chapel Hill.

Atlantic Coast Line Railroad employees stand outside the freight office in the late 1800s. Courtesy of the North Carolina Collection, UNC Library, Chapel Hill.

On April 28, 1891, the steamer *Wilmington* came up the Cape Fear River with flags flying and blew her whistle to announce her arrival at the wharf in Wilmington. An iron steamer, she carried 500 passengers and was owned by Captain John W. Harper. Her initial run was to the city of Southport below Wilmington. The *Wilmington* made excursions fifteen miles downriver to the popular resort of Carolina Beach, discharging passengers at the pier where they boarded railroad cars to the beach. Courtesy of the North Carolina State Archives.

A well-dressed couple relaxes on the promenade of the steamer *Wilmington*. Passengers had access to two saloons on the main and upper decks and to a handsome and roomy cabin. Courtesy of the Lower Cape Fear Historical Society.

Police Officers Foltz (left) and Kendrick show off their bloodhounds Kate (left) and John around 1900. Founded in 1739, the Wilmington Police Department was called "The Watch." A Black Maria drawn by a horse and with a foot-operated gong on the floor was used to pick up drunks and troublemakers and take them to jail. Courtesy of the New Hanover County Public Library.

Opposite page:
A tightrope walker drew large crowds on Market Street in the late 1800s. At the end of Market Street, the old Market House stood between Water and Front streets. It was demolished in 1881 and was replaced with the Market House on South Front Street between Dock and Orange Streets. A horse-drawn trolley is in the center of the picture on the unpaved street. Courtesy of the New Hanover County Museum.

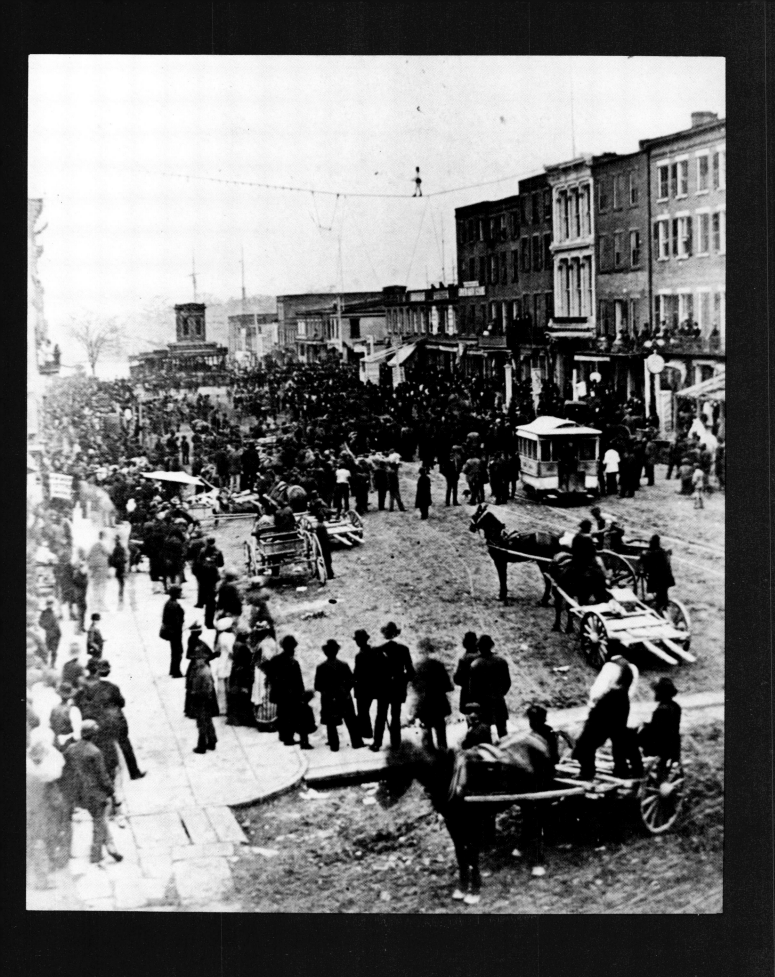

These produce wagons were lined up at the corner of Front and Dock streets around 1900. The Market House on South Front Street between Dock and Orange streets was built just before the old Market House at the foot of Market Street was demolished in 1881. Courtesy of the North Carolina State Archives.

Ox-carts were among the varied means of transportation which were a part of the Wilmington scene in the late 1800s. Courtesy of the New Hanover County Museum.

In the late 1800s, Tom Quinlivan, horseshoer and farrier, operated this blacksmith shop at the corner of Third and Princess streets near City Hall and Thalian Hall. Wilmington horses were shoed at Quinlivan's, stabled at Orrell's Stables, and watered at "Horse Pond" near the corner of Front and Grace streets. From the James McKoy Collection; courtesy of Thalian Hall.

J. W. Murchison was a student at the Cape Fear Academy, 1864-1869. The school was founded by General R. E. Colston and was attended by the sons of prominent families. The Murchison family owned Murchison National Bank. From the Julian Martin Collection; courtesy of the Lower Cape Fear Historical Society.

Alex Sprunt (standing) and Fred deRosset (sitting) were students at the Cape Fear Academy from 1864 to 1869. The Sprunt family owned shipping interests and the largest cotton export business in America, known as Alexander Sprunt and Son. Their residence was at Ninth and Princess streets. The deRosset family had donated the property for St. John's Episcopal Church in 1853 at the corner of Third and Red Cross streets. From the Julian Martin Collection; courtesy of the Lower Cape Fear Historical Society.

Brooke Empie (seated) and William Love Moore (left) pose with a friend in baseball costumes of the late 1800s. The Empie family came to Wilmington when the Reverend Adam Empie, first chaplain of the United States Military Academy at West Point, in 1814, was called to be rector of St. James Episcopal Church. From the Pickrell Collection; courtesy of the Lower Cape Fear Historical Society.

This picture of the Temple of Israel was made in 1890, fifteen years after the cornerstone was laid at the corner of Fourth and Market streets. The ceremonies included an address by Colonel A. M. Waddell, a former Congressman who later became mayor. The rabbi at this time was Samuel Mendelsohn. The Temple of Israel congregation was made up of German Jews who had emigrated to Wilmington around 1840 and had become well established in the city. Families associated with the Temple include the Bluethenthals, the Dannenbaums, the Jacobis, and the Bears. The Jewish Reform cemetery is a part of Oakdale cemetery and is encircled with a fence ornamented with a Star of David.

The B'nai Israel Synagogue on Chestnut Street was established around 1912 by East European Jewish immigrants who arrived in Wilmington at the turn of the century. Family names associated with this congregation are Schwartz, Kingoff, D'Lugia, and Block. Courtesy of the North Carolina State Archives.

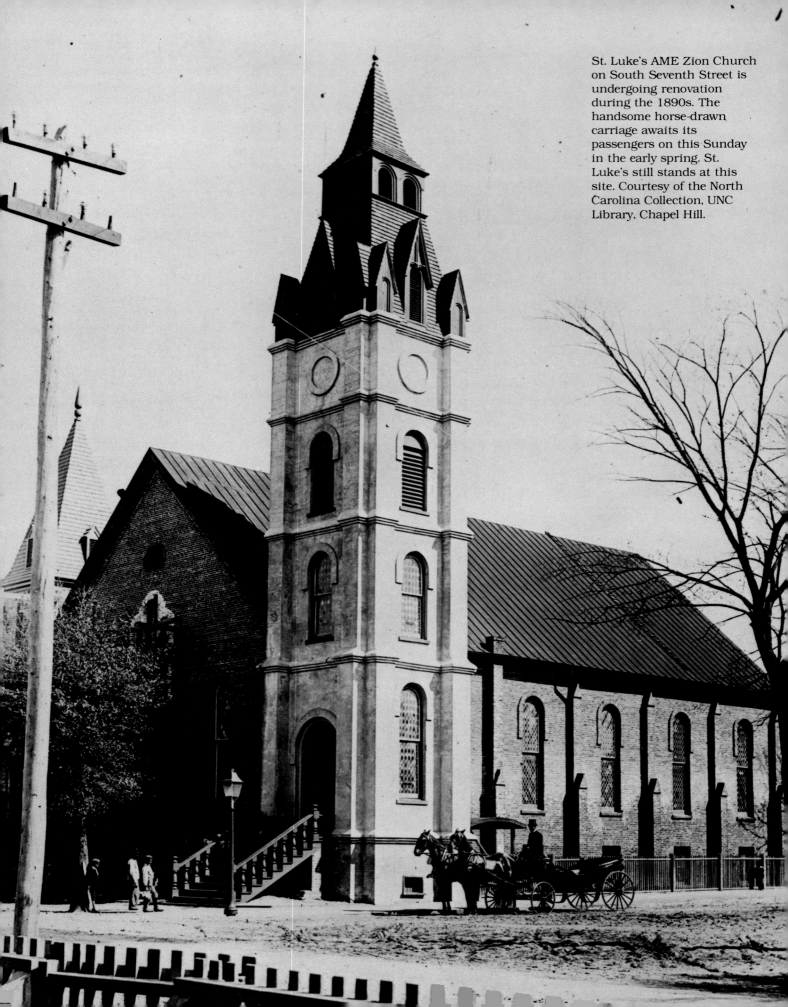

St. Luke's AME Zion Church on South Seventh Street is undergoing renovation during the 1890s. The handsome horse-drawn carriage awaits its passengers on this Sunday in the early spring. St. Luke's still stands at this site. Courtesy of the North Carolina Collection, UNC Library, Chapel Hill.

The old YMCA on North Front Street between Grace and Walnut streets was completed in 1891. The Young Men's Christian Association met in the Masonic building on Market Street first, and then on the second floor of the Bank of New Hanover until revivals conducted by evangelist R. G. Pearson in 1888 raised funds for a YMCA building. Thousands of people attended the revivals, held in a corner wareroom of the Champion Compress Company at Walnut and Nutt streets. The J. Hicks Bunting Drug Company can be seen on the first floor of the YMCA, its windows displaying a full line of pharmaceuticals and toiletries. Courtesy of the *Wilmington Star-News.*

This picture of the YMCA on Market Street near Third Street was taken on a warm summer day not long after the building was constructed in 1913. In front of the YMCA is a monument to the Honorable George Davis, Attorney-General of the Confederacy. Courtesy of the North Carolina Collection, UNC Library, Chapel Hill.

71

Woodrow Wilson plaque erected by the Daughters of the American Revolution in 1929 in the vestibule of the First Presbyterian Church, of which President Wilson was a member. Woodrow Wilson resided in Wilmington with his parents during the summer of 1874 and for some time thereafter, in a house at the southeast corner of Front and Nun streets and later at the Presbyterian manse at Fourth and Orange streets.

A student at Davidson College, "Tommy" Wilson, as he was then known, suffered from a digestive disorder. His father purchased for him the first high wheel bicycle in Wilmington in hopes that it would improve his health. Riding the bicycle down the steep incline of Orange Street, Wilson is said to have gone headlong into the Cape Fear River.

Wilson was fascinated with the docks on the river and would obtain permission from the pilots to board outgoing vessels, returning to Wilmington on pilot boats. He attended courts in session in Wilmington and would take afternoon strolls with his mother in the shade of South Third Street. In a letter to John D. Sprunt, President Wilson said, "My thoughts often go back to the days in Wilmington." Courtesy of the North Carolina State Archives.

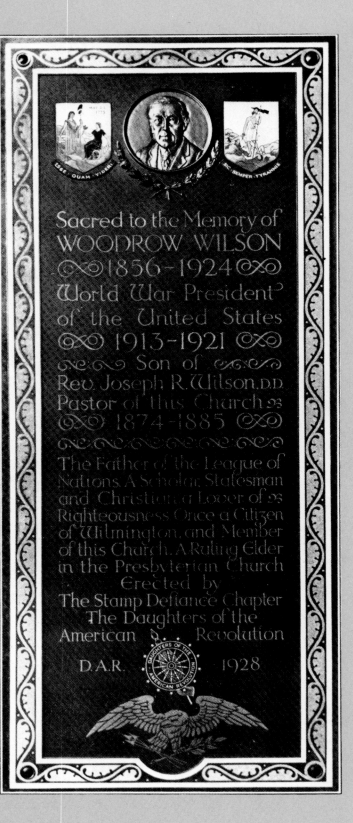

Sacred to the Memory of
WOODROW WILSON
1856–1924
World War President
of the United States
1913–1921
Son of
Rev. Joseph R. Wilson, D.D.
Pastor of this Church
1874–1885

The Father of the League of Nations, A Scholar, Statesman and Christian, a Lover of Righteousness Once a Citizen of Wilmington, and Member of this Church, A Ruling Elder in the Presbyterian Church
Erected by
The Stamp Defiance Chapter
The Daughters of the
American Revolution

D.A.R.   1928

Robert R. Bellamy established his wholesale and retail drug business in 1885, specializing in the preparation of "physicians' prescriptions and family recipes." The stock of the store and warehouse included all patent medicines and toilet articles. Courtesy of the North Carolina State Archives.

The R. R. Bellamy residence in the 500 block of Market Street was photographed around 1900. Robert R. Bellamy carried on a wholesale and retail drug business and was an officer in other Wilmington businesses, such as the Delgado Mills, the Carolina Insurance Company, and the North Carolina Building and Loan Association. Courtesy of the North Carolina State Archives.

H. A. Tucker and Brother marble and granite works on North Front Street was founded in the late 1800s by H. A. and R. D. Tucker. No longer at this location, the firm supplied the stone for the Murchison National Bank in Wilmington and for mausoleum and monuments for the Murchison, Vollers, Love, and Worth families in Oakdale cemetery. Twenty skilled workers were employed in the business. Courtesy of the North Carolina Collection, UNC Library, Chapel Hill.

J. H. Rehder and Company on North Front Street was established in 1887 as a wholesale and retail dry goods business which supplied the "latest in New York and Paris designs," as well as "anything dealt in by the country merchants." The windows in this picture taken around 1900 display the wide variety of merchandise available to the Wilmington public, including men's and women's clothing and articles for the home. Courtesy of the North Carolina Collection, UNC Library, Chapel Hill.

The Racket Store was founded in 1888 by George Gaylord on North Front Street. In this picture taken in 1902, the employees of the department store gather on the sidewalk to display merchandise. Wearing apparel, furniture, trunks, carpets, and candy were sold, and a large mail order business was conducted. Courtesy of the North Carolina State Archives.

The Home Brewing Company advertised home beer at its Wilmington branch on North Water Street at the turn of the century. The Richmond-based brewery produced malt beverages, with the Wilmington establishment consisting of a warehouse and bottling works under management by J. M. Wright. Courtesy of the North Carolina Collection, UNC Library, Chapel Hill.

The exports of the Express Steamboat Company out of Wilmington in 1882 included cotton, lumber, turpentine, rice, yarn and peanuts. Imports were sugar, liquor, coffee, brick, shoes, hay, and bacon. In this same year, the old Market House at the foot of Market Street was torn down and replaced by the new Market House between Dock and Orange streets. Courtesy of the New Hanover County Museum.

The imports and exports by this line of first class steamers for the year 1882 were as follows:

EXPORTS.

Cotton, bales,	58,655.	Rice, meal, sacks,	4,396.
Lumber, feet,	5,640,707.	" rough, "	4,131.
Shooks,	2,935.	Molasses, hhds,	130.
Shingles,	1,292,000.	Peanuts, sacks,	1,197.
Naval Stores, bbls,	95,607.	Pig Iron, tons,	174.
Spirits Turpentine "	27,400.	Yarn, bales,	366.
Rice, cleaned, tcs,	3,950.	Merchandise, pkgs,	7,676.

IMPORTS.

Syrup, bbls,	1,379.	Ties, bundles,	3,162.
Sugar, "	6,195.	Bagging, rolls,	15,875.
Bacon, boxes,	10,318.	Cement, bbls,	600.
Lard, pkgs,	1,570.	Water Pipe, pieces,	916.
Corn, sacks,	114,503.	Brick,	10,200.
Oats, "	7,251.	Sulphur, tons,	437.
Hay, bales,	25,328.	Railroad Iron, rails,	2,785.
Liquor, pkgs,	686.	Merchandize, pkgs,	143,601
Oil(lubricating only)		Shoes, cases,	3,776.
bbls,	144.	Barrels, empty,	21,346.
Coffee, sacks,	5,913.	Guano, sacks,	40,510.

EXPRESS STEAMBOAT COMPANY.—CAPITAL $50,000.

WILMINGTON AND FAYETTEVILLE.

	CAPACITY.	COST.	
"D. Murchison,"	1,000 barrels.	$22,000.	Iron Hull
"Wave,"	800 "	13,000.	" "

The Frank A. Thompson Company was one of several firms engaged in the turpentine industry at Wilmington. The Spirittine Chemical Company and the George L. Morton Comany on Nutt Street also manufactured spirits of turpentine, rosin, and pitch for shipment to paint dealers, varnish manufacturers, ship chandlers, and steel works. Courtesy of the New Hanover County Museum.

76

A turpentine still at Wilmington in the early 1900s shows the many barrels produced by the industry. Photograph by C.W. Yates and Company; courtesy of the North Carolina Collection, UNC Library, Chapel Hill.

A TURPEN

The offices of the Spirittine Chemical Company, distillers and refiners of pitch pine products, were photographed during the Depression. Founded in 1890 by L. Hanson, the factory was at the foot of Dawson Street. Spirittine Wood Preserver was the primary product of the company. It was used to preserve ships' timbers, telegraph poles and railroad ties. Other products were Pure Pine Oil and Sheep Dip. Courtesy of the New Hanover County Public Library.

Workers in the turpentine industry bleed a pine tree of rosin for use in the manufacture of industrial products. Black labor was used extensively for this work in the 1800s. Courtesy of the New Hanover County Public Library.

Pine logs are heated to recover rosin for use in the turpentine industry in Wilmington during the Depression. Courtesy of the New Hanover County Public Library.

A paddle wheel steamer loads rosin at a dock on Water Street at the Cape Fear River. Behind the steamer is a warehouse of Worth and Worth, a large shipping business established in 1852 by T. C. and B. G. Worth, brothers. The firm served as agents for the Cape Fear Steamboat Company. Vessels built by the Worths include the *Flora McDonald*, the *A. P. Hurt*, and the *Governor Worth*. Courtesy of the North Carolina State Archives.

The Navassa Guano Company was established in 1869 with an office on North Water Street and two large plants nearby, Navassa Station and Almont. Shown in this picture around 1900, the Navassa Station factory was four miles south of Wilmington on the Cape Fear River, employing 362 people. A total of 60,000 tons of fertilizer was manufactured annually at Navassa from phosphate rock, ammoniate, and potash salts for use on tobacco, cotton, and vegetable crops. Almont produced 30,000 tons each year. Today the Royster, Smith-Douglass, Swift and USS Agri-Chemicals fertilizer companies are located at Navassa. Courtesy of the North Carolina Collection, UNC Library, Chapel Hill.

Rafts of lumber float in the Cape Fear River around 1890. Courtesy of the North Carolina State Archives.

Three-masted barks load naval stores and groceries at the docks of D. McEachern on North Water Street in the 1890s. The wholesale grocer carried pickled meats, corn, flour, molasses, tobacco, and sugar, as well as naval stores. Establishing his business in 1893, McEachern was president of the Cape Fear and Peoples' Steamboat Company and Chairman of the Board of County Commissioners. Courtesy of the North Carolina Collection, UNC Library, Chapel Hill.

The busy wharves at Wilmington at the turn of the century utilized four-masted schooners, railroad cars, and river steamers as the smoke of various industries rose in the air above the Cape Fear River. Courtesy of the North Carolina Collection, UNC Library, Chapel Hill.

A three-masted schooner and a two-masted schooner out of Annapolis, Maryland, load lumber at the Wilmington docks on the Cape Fear River in the late 1800s. A number of lumber companies did business in Wilmington, among them the Kidder Lumber Company, established in 1839 by Gilbert Potter and Edward Kidder, and the Hilton Lumber Company, founded in 1856 by O. G. Parsley. The Cape Fear Lumber Company was organized around 1900, and the Angola Lumber Company shortly thereafter. Pine and cypress were the principal woods exported. Courtesy of the North Carolina Collection, UNC Library, Chapel Hill.

The Clyde Steamship
Company wharf adjoined the
dock of the Champion
Compress and Warehouse
Company in 1900. Clyde
steamers ran between New
York and Georgetown, South
Carolina, as painted on the
stern of the vessel in this
photograph. The steamship
George W. Clyde weighed
1574 tons, one of a fleet of
ships with passenger
accommodations. H. G.
Smallbones was the
superintendent of the
company in Wilmington.
Courtesy of the North
Carolina Collection, UNC
Library, Chapel Hill.

A BIRD'S EYE VIEW OF ONE OF WILMINGTON'S LEADING INDUSTRIES.

Br. BARQUE "GEORGE DAVIS,"
For HAVRE, FRANCE.

Br. S. S. "ROSEVILLE,"
For REVAL, RUSSIA.

Br. S. S "PENSHER,"
For BREMEN, GERMANY.

Br. S. S. "DALBEATTIE,"
For LIVERPOOL, ENGLAND.

View of Vessels Loading by ALEXANDER SPRUNT & SON, at the Wharves of the CHAMPION COMPRESS AND WAREHOUSE COMPANY, Wilmington, N. C.

Four vessels load cotton at the wharves of the Champion Compress and Warehouse Company of Alexander Sprunt and Son in the late 1800s. The *George Davis* would sail for Havre, France; the *Roseville* for Reval, Russia; the *Pensher* for Bremen, Germany; and the *Dalbeattie* for Liverpool, England. Courtesy of the North Carolina State Archives.

These interior views of Alexander Sprunt and Son show activities of the largest single cotton handling firm in the United States at the turn of the century. The direct agencies extended from Barcelona and Genoa on the Mediterranean, to Helsingfors in the Gulf of Finland and Moscow in central Russia. Offices were in Wilmington and Liverpool, England, and Bremen, Germany.

The warehouses had a complete system of automatic sprinklers in case of fire, and the buildings covered two city blocks, with a storage capacity of 25,000 bales of cotton. The Sprunt firm pioneered the steam foreign trade in Wilmington, chartering the first steamer, the *Barnesmore*, in 1881, and previously shipping naval stores on sailing vessels after becoming established in 1866. Alexander Sprunt died in 1884, leaving the business to his sons, James Sprunt and William Sprunt. Courtesy of the North Carolina Collection, UNC Library, Chapel Hill.

A cotton ship, the *Jessmore*, loads for export at the Champion Compress wharves in 1902. The Champion Compress, under the presidency of E.J. Pennypacker, and the Wilmington Compress, under George W. Williams, were merged into the cotton export business of Alexander Sprunt and Son, the largest single cotton handling firm in the United States. In 1898, 318,450 bales of cotton were shipped from Wilmington. Courtesy of the North Carolina State Archives.

Amy Morris Bradley came to Wilmington from New England and began the Tileston Normal School in 1872, living in a cottage on Ann Street in the Tileston Schoolyard. Miss Bradley served as principal of Tileston School for twenty years. From the album of A.O. McEachern; gift of Mrs. Lena McCarley and Mrs. A. A. Griffin; courtesy of the Lower Cape Fear Historical Society.

Faithfully Yours
Amy M. Bradley.

Mary Tileston Hemenway was the benefactress of Tileston School. From New England, Hemenway made possible the work of Amy Bradley in establishing public schools in Wilmington. Hemenway School and Tileston School were named after the generous educator. From the album of A. O. McEachern; gift of Mrs. Lena McCarley and Mrs. A. A. Griffin; courtesy of the Lower Cape Fear Historical Society.

Amy Bradley, Principal of Tileston Normal School, can be seen on the left side of this picture behind two of her teachers, wearing her dark, high-necked dress with the prim white collar and looking over her charges on a warm spring day. This photograph was taken in the 1880s. Courtesy of the New Hanover County Museum.

Amy Bradley's cottage was a small, brown dwelling on the grounds of Tileston High School. After Miss Bradley's death in 1904, the cottage was used as a student club house and as a residence for principals of the school. It is no longer in existence. From the Emma Woodward MacMillan Collection; courtesy of James Alfred Miller.

Tileston School is presently an elementary school. In this picture of the structure on Ann Street, the original school building can be seen covered with vines at the rear of the addition. Courtesy of the North Carolina Collection, UNC Library, Chapel Hill.

Hemenway School on Fourth Street between Red Cross and Campbell streets was a part of the graded school system of Wilmington in the 1880s, along with Union School, Peabody School, and Williston School. Professor M. C. S. Noble worked hard during this period to establish the system. He was subsequently appointed Professor of Pedagogy at the University of North Carolina and was succeeded in Wilmington by Professor John J. Blair. Courtesy of the North Carolina Collection, UNC Library, Chapel Hill.

Opposite page:
The Union Free School was constructed in 1857 on South Sixth Street between Nun and Church streets, using funds raised by subscription. In 1867, Amy Bradley began her educational work in the Union schoolhouse, where she taught until she moved into the new Tileston School in 1872. Courtesy of the North Carolina Collection, UNC Library, Chapel Hill.

These schoolchildren of 1894 include Anna Parsley, Nellie Cotchett, Virginia Bailey, Atha Hicks, Robert Bridgers, Bessie Latimer, Annabel Latimer, and Julia Worth. Children of the Scott, Hall, Burress, and McQueen families are also present. Courtesy of the Lower Cape Fear Historical Society.

This photograph of Union School was made around 1900. Courtesy of the North Carolina State Archives.

The Wilmington Fire
Department shows off its
equipment in the early
1900s. Horse-drawn trucks
take a back seat to the shiny
new motor-driven fire
engines. City officials join
members of the fire
department at this proud
moment. Fire was such a
dangerous reality for the city
of Wilmington that
equipment and personnel
were kept in top condition
in case of crisis. Courtesy of
the Wilmington Fire
Department.

Charles Schnibben was the
first chief of the Wilmington
Fire Department. In 1856, a
group of Germans and
Irishmen organized the
Howard Relief Steam Fire
Engine Company in
Wilmington as a volunteer
service. The Rankin Steam
Company and the
Wilmington Hook and
Ladder Company were also
formed. In 1897, the first
fully paid fire department
was officially recognized by
the City. German-born
Schnibben was named chief
at this time, at the age of
thirty. Eighteen Negroes and
twelve Caucasians made up
the fire department.
Courtesy of the Wilmington
Fire Department.

"FAITHFUL UNTO DEATH."

This monument in Oakdale Cemetery commemorates the deaths of Captain William Ellerbrook and his faithful dog Boss, who gave up his life in an effort to drag his master from a burning building at the corner of Front and Dock streets in 1880. Captain Ellerbrook was master of a Heide Company tugboat, and he answered the call to save the burning store. Caught by falling timbers, Ellerbrook was killed. Before his death, his dog Boss heard his screams for help and dashed into the burning building, only to be found the next day beside Ellerbrook's body with a piece of cloth torn from his master's coat still in his mouth. The dog was buried in the casket with Captain Ellerbrook in a funeral attended by hundreds of Wilmington citizens. Courtesy of the Wilmington Fire Department.

This placard lists the location of fire alarm boxes in Wilmington in 1886, the year of the disastrous waterfront fire which destroyed much of the downtown area. Beginning at the river at the foot of Chestnut Street, the fire swept along the east bank of the river burning wharves, warehouses, and stores. Martial law was declared. Courtesy of the Wilmington Fire Department.

Location Fire Alarm Boxes.

GAMEWELL SYSTEM.

BROOKLYN.

	No.	Strikes
4th and Brunswick,	31	3—1
7th and Harnett,	25	2—5
C. C. Depot, B'nsw'k & Nutt	13	1—3

CITY NORTH OF MARKET ST.

	No.	Strikes
3rd and Princess—City Hall	14	1—4
Mulberry and Front	15	1—5
7th and Mulberry	16	1—6
Market and Water	24	2—4
8th and Market	35	3—5
6th and Red Cross	43	4—3

CITY SOUTH OF MARKET ST.

	No.	Strikes
Front and Orange	21	2—1
7th and Queen	23	2—3
3rd and Nun	32	3—2
Front and Castle	34	3—4
5th and Castle	41	4—1
5th and Orange	42	4—2

CHAS. D. MYERS,
Chief Fire Dep't.

Wilmington, N. C., April 1st, 1886.

DeRosset & Meares, Printers to the City.

Fire Alarm Boxes 1886

Dynamite launch docked in the Cape Fear River in front of the U. S. Customs House in 1898. A small attack boat developed by the U. S. Navy as a forerunner of the destroyer, the dynamite launch carried a torpedo. Here the crew has taken advantage of Wilmington's safe harbor to hang out their laundry to dry. Courtesy of the Lower Cape Fear Historical Society.

Alexander Manly was the editor of the black newspaper in Wilmington, the *Daily Record*, when the offices of this paper were burned during the 1898 Race Riots. The *Daily Record* was the only black newspaper in the United States which published on a daily basis. The race riots occurred at 1 p.m. on Thursday, November 10, 1898, two days after election. Editor Manly had earlier written an editorial pointing out the abuse of black women by white men. This article helped stir up the riot, which resulted in the deaths of seven blacks and the destruction of the *Daily Record*. Manly escaped from Wilmington, aided by his appearance of being white.

Prominent black officeholders and professionals in Wilmington at this time included John Dancy, customs collector; David Jacobs, county coroner; Dan Howard, jailer; John Howe, legislator; Armand W. Scott, lawyer; Dr. T. R. Mask, physician; Fred Sadgwar, financier and architect; R. S. Pickens, magistrate; Thomas Rivera, mortician; David J. Jones, wheelwright; and J. W. Telfair, manager of the James Sprunt Cotton Press. Courtesy of Felice Sadgwar.

Opposite Page:

The Shell Road curved through bowers of live oaks and evergreen pines, its oyster shells bleached white. The hard surface of the road was a blessing for vehicles, animals, and passengers, and the beauty of the road made it famous throughout the Carolinas. The road was opened in 1876 and is now a modern highway for which no tolls are charged. Courtesy of the North Carolina Collection, UNC Library, Chapel Hill.

The last Republican governor of North Carolina prior to James Holshouser in 1972, Daniel L. Russell was governor during the period of the 1898 Race Riots in Wilmington. Governor Russell's residence stood at the corner of Dock and Second streets. Courtesy of the *Wilmington Star-News.*

The Shell Road at Myrtle Court. Now known as Wrightsville Avenue, the original road was built by the Wilmington and Coast Turnpike Company of rock and shells. The route ran from Seventeenth and Dock streets parallel to Burnt Mill Creek, across Greenville Road and Bradley's Creek to Wrightsville Sound. From the Julian Martin Collection; courtesy of the Lower Cape Fear Historical Society.

A toll stop on the Shell Road at the turn of the century. A horse-drawn vehicle called a wagonette made daily runs from the Orrell livery stables in downtown Wilmington. Toll houses punched tickets and collected fees from travelers. Courtesy of the Lower Cape Fear Historical Society.

Harbor Island as it appeared in 1926, looking toward Wrightsville Beach. Also known as The Hammocks, Mary Island, and Shore Acres at different stages of development, Harbor Island was opened on July 1, 1888, with a footbridge and the Island Beach Hotel. The low-lying island of dunes, sea oats, and green marsh was a retreat for thousands of white cranes which nested in the twisted live oaks. Courtesy of the New Hanover County Public Library.

The Big Storm of 1899, a hurricane which struck just before dawn on November 1 of that year, left the massive Sea Coast Railroad trestle leading to the Hammocks and Wrightsville Beach a tangled wreck in the waters of the sound J. T. Dooley, section master of the W&SC Railroad, left the Hammocks with his wife and children at 3:30 a.m., and at 4 a.m. waves demolished the trestle over which the Dooley family had just passed. From the Pickrell Collection; courtesy of the Lower Cape Fear Historical Society.

The Carolina Yacht Club was severely damaged in the Big Storm of 1899 and had to be rebuilt. A number of cottages belonging to Wilmington families, among them Emerson, Bridgers, Murchison, Parsley, and Strange, were destroyed or completely carried away. From the Pickrell Collection; courtesy of the Lower Cape Fear Historical Society.

James Walker Memorial Hospital was completed in 1901 at a site in the northeastern section of Wilmington known as Klein's Gardens, where the old City Hospital stood. The new medical facility was given to the city by local builder James Walker, who died shortly before the structure was completed. Dr. William J. H. Bellamy inspired Walker to make a gift of the hospital. Wilmington citizens were born, operated upon, nursed back to health, and ministered to at death in the rambling facility until it was replaced by New Hanover Memorial Hospital on South Seventeenth Street in 1967. Photograph by C. W. Yates and Company; courtesy of the North Carolina Collection, UNC Library, Chapel Hill.

THE TURN OF THE CENTURY

The twentieth century brought a period of prosperity to Wilmington after it had survived war, pestilence, fires, earthquake, blizzards, and racial conflict during the preceding years. Five railroads terminated at Wilmington, steamships plied its waters, and the town boasted electric lights, telephones, a waterworks, and an ice plant. As if to set the pace for the decades of progress and equilibrium to follow, on May 22, 1900, the first brick was laid for James Walker Memorial Hospital, an institution which would serve Wilmington's citizens from birth to death and in which the city took great pride.

In 1909, the citizens put on a grand display for a distinguished visitor, President William Howard Taft, who made an address from a stand in front of City Hall on November 9. Welcoming banners, a grand procession, an honor guard, and a lavish dinner at the home of James Sprunt on Front Street ornamented the occasion. As the largest city in the state with a population of 25,000, Wilmington was determined to show itself to best advantage.

New buildings were erected. In 1912, the new station and office building of the Atlantic Coast Line Railroad and the new YMCA on Market Street near Third Street were begun. In 1916, contracts were awarded for the new Customs House on Water Street. Wooden sidewalks raised pedestrians above the level of the street, where horse leavings made the going hazardous for the well-attired. Sixty saloons did a thriving business until state prohibition caused them to be closed in 1909.

The rich farmlands surrounding the city of Wilmington were developed by Hugh MacRae, who established the Castle Hayne farm colony north of the city and brought hard-working, frugal, sturdy European immigrants of several nationalities to the Cape Fear area. The farm colonies prospered, becoming an example of good planning and skilled agricultural techniques.

Wilmington citizens enjoyed themselves. They played a variety of sports, establishing football teams and golf tournaments. The vacation homes at the sound became meccas of social activity. Oyster roasts and dances were frequent. The trolley line to Wrightsville Beach brought hordes of people to the fine hotels and to the magnificent Lumina Pavilion which had been constructed in 1905 by the Tidewater Power Company. A major attraction was the huge movie screen on tall pilings at the edge of the ocean, where hundreds of viewers could sit in an outdoor theater and watch the stars of Hollywood under the stars of Wrightsville Beach.

In 1917, the First World War interrupted the comfortable existence. Two German merchant ships were captured in Wilmington harbor, and members of the Wilmington Light Infantry left to fight in France in Battery C, Second Battalion, Trench Artillery. The Carolina and Liberty shipyards were opened, and the first concrete ship built in North Carolina was named the *Cape Fear* at launching. The first steel ship, the *Cranford,* was launched. In 1919, the German submarine *U-117* was brought to Wilmington as a trophy, lying at the wharf at the foot of Princess Street for the townspeople to examine. In 1918, an influenza epidemic had taken 120 lives. In 1919, thirty of Wilmington's World War I soldiers did not return home with their buddies, lying dead in foreign soil.

While World War I had been disruptive, it had also brought prosperity to the city with the activity at the shipyards. The victory of the Allies brought much celebration among Wilmington's citizens, who entered the Roaring Twenties with money in their pockets and enthusiasm in their hearts.

This turn-of-the-century picture shows the steamer *Wilmington* in port at Water Street between Market and Princess streets. The tall building in the center at the river's edge is believed to be the original Customs House. Courtesy of the North Carolina State Archives.

The City Hospital was founded in 1881 at the corner of Tenth and Red Cross streets on property known as Klein's Gardens. Plank sidewalks above the mud of the streets led pedestrians to the hospital when they did not have the benefit of horse and carriage. Physicians at the hospital included Dr. William J. Love, Dr. W. J. H. Bellamy, Dr. A. H. Harriss, and Dr. R. D. Jewett. City Hospital was replaced with James Walker Memorial Hospital in 1901. Courtesy of Hubert Eaton.

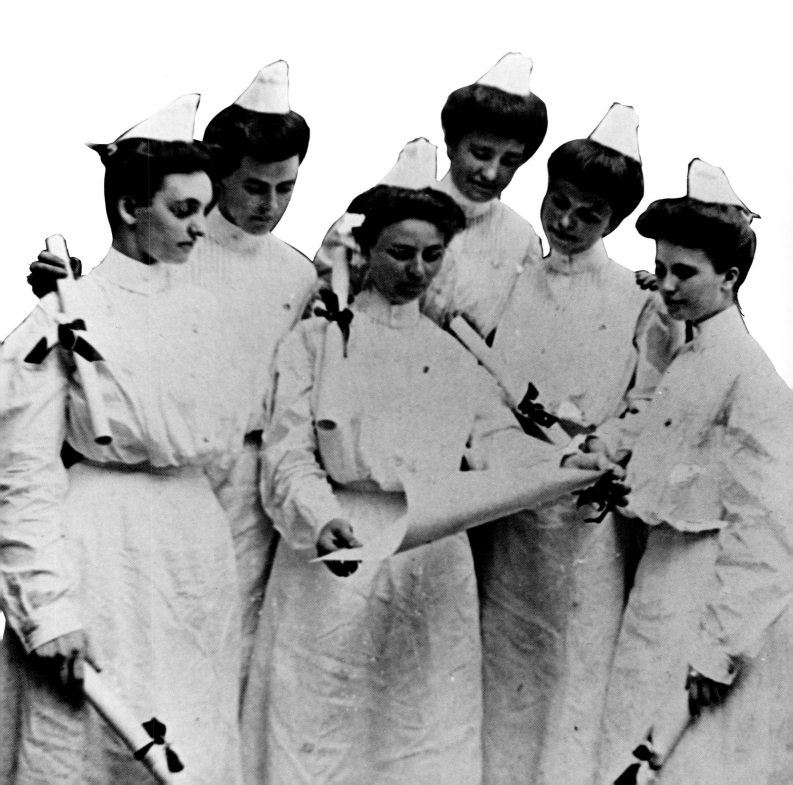

An early graduating class of nurses at James Walker Memorial Hospital wear the uniforms of angels of mercy and admire their hard-won diplomas. Among those pictured here are Bessie McCord, Bertha Cromarti, and Lola Compton. Courtesy of the New Hanover County Museum.

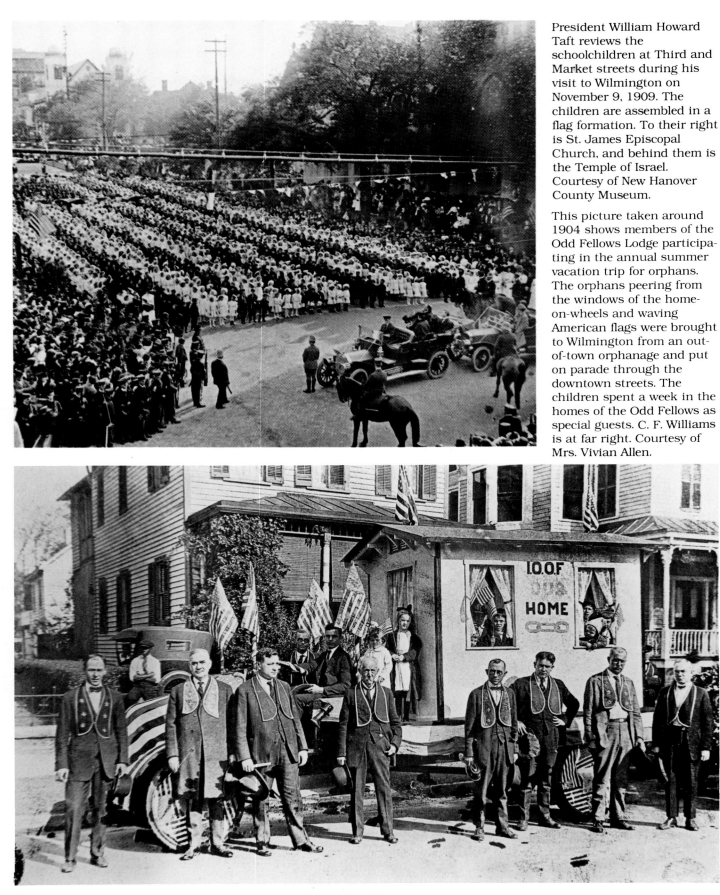

President William Howard Taft reviews the schoolchildren at Third and Market streets during his visit to Wilmington on November 9, 1909. The children are assembled in a flag formation. To their right is St. James Episcopal Church, and behind them is the Temple of Israel. Courtesy of New Hanover County Museum.

This picture taken around 1904 shows members of the Odd Fellows Lodge participating in the annual summer vacation trip for orphans. The orphans peering from the windows of the home-on-wheels and waving American flags were brought to Wilmington from an out-of-town orphanage and put on parade through the downtown streets. The children spent a week in the homes of the Odd Fellows as special guests. C. F. Williams is at far right. Courtesy of Mrs. Vivian Allen.

Mrs. Rufus W. Hicks was the founder of the North Carolina Sorosis, which promotes art in the public schools and art appreciation among its members. Established in 1895, the Sorosis has supported many cultural activities in Wilmington, including the New Hanover County Museum. From *Two Centuries of Art in New Hanover County*; courtesy of Crockette Hewlett.

President William Howard Taft visited Wilmington on November 9, 1909. The people of the Port City erected a huge welcome arch on Front Street in front of the Post Office. Stores and residences were decorated with banners. A crowd of more than 15,000 gathered for the grand procession and the President's address from a stand erected at City Hall. Taft was entertained at the home of James Sprunt on the corner of Front and Nun streets. The presidential party made a trip down the Cape Fear River on the revenue cutter *Seminole*. The North Carolina militia under the command of Colonel John Van B. Metts took part in the ceremonies, and the Wilmington Light Infantry formed the special bodyguard. Courtesy of the North Carolina Collection, UNC Library, Chapel Hill.

...ellows Temple, Princess Street,
...ing East, Wilmington, N. C.

The Odd Fellows Temple on Princess Street is across from Orrell's Livery and Stables in this picture taken in 1907. The Odd Fellows Lodge was organized in 1842 over a grain store on Water Street. In 1843, the lodge established a school at Fourth and Princess streets under principal Robert McLaughlin, who was red-haired, had a cork leg, and believed in liberal use of the hickory stick. Courtesy of the North Carolina State Archives.

In 1900, the Carolina Central Railway became a part of the Seaboard Air Line Railroad, whose yard is shown in this picture. Thomas D. Meares was the Wilmington agent for SAL. The railroad offered passenger service as well as freight service for the many commodities produced in Wilmington and transported to points north, west, and south. Courtesy of the North Carolina Collection, UNC Library, Chapel Hill.

Strawberry pickers on the farms at Castle Hayne show off their harvesting technique around 1905. Strawberries were the most successful crop, with 331,360 crates shipped in refrigerator cars from Wilmington in 1901. The Atlantic Coast Line and Seaboard Air Line railroads carried the berries to New York, New England, and as far north as Toronto. Courtesy of the North Carolina Collection, UNC Library, Chapel Hill.

A farm family near Wilmington shows off its strawberry harvest around 1928. As the women pack the berries into cartons in the shade of the shed, the children proudly stand beside the crop they have helped transport in their wagon. The Castle Hayne Colony originally consisted of about forty families of Dutch, Hungarians and Poles. North of Wilmington at St. Helena, fifty families included Austrians, Russians, and North Italians. The small farms, rarely over twenty acres each, were owned by the families and were debt-free. Courtesy of the New Hanover County Public Library.

The Tinga Nursery at Castle Hayne presently grows evergreens and ornamental trees and shrubs. When this picture was taken in the late 1920s, the thirty-acre farm was known for its tulip production. The Dutch bulb-growers who settled at Wilmington were highly successful with their flowers. Courtesy of the New Hanover County Public Library.

In the late 1920s, flower growers in Castle Hayne show off their abundant crop. The Castle Hayne farm colony was established in the early 1900s by Hugh MacRae. Ten- and twenty-acre farms were created, provided with roads and drainage, and sold to European immigrants. An experienced farm superintendent instructed the newly arrived farmers in preparation of the land, selection of seeds and fertilizers, and cultivation and marketing of crops. In 1927, a commission appointed by the United States secretary of the interior stated that "the most impressive demonstration of what is possible in the South which the advisers have seen are the farm colonies near Wilmington, North Carolina, developed under the guidance and with the substantial financial assistance of Hugh MacRae." Courtesy of the New Hanover County Public Library.

The lettuce beds on the famous Sans Souci truck farm two miles outside Wilmington covered seven acres. Lettuce was grown under canvas in the winter and in the open in the spring, bringing from 250 to 300 dollars an acre around 1910, when this picture was taken. Radishes, asparagus, peas, beans, cabbages, and potatoes were other lucrative crops. Courtesy of the North Carolina Collection, UNC Library, Chapel Hill.

Anna Mathilda McNeill Whistler, better known as "Whistler's Mother," was born September 27, 1804, in Wilmington to Dr. Daniel McNeill and Martha Kingsley McNeill. The subject of "Arrangement in Grey and Black No. 1: the Artist's Mother," by James McNeill Whistler, lived in the family home at the southwest corner of Fourth and Orange streets until she was ten years old. Anna McNeill Whistler returned to Wilmington during the Civil War and embarked on the blockade runner *Advance* to visit her son in London. Because of the perilous times, she carried with her a special letter from Governor Z.B. Vance granting her permission to sail on the ship. She is buried in Hastings, England, with an inscription on her tombstone which states that she was born in Wilmington, North Carolina. Courtesy of Elizabeth Russell.

The Delgado Mills was established in 1899 to manufacture cotton fabrics such as madras and seersucker from Mississippi and Alabama long staple cotton. These fabrics were used in shirts and blouses, children's dresses, and aprons. The entire company plant occupied 101 acres off Wrightsville Avenue, with 97 houses, a church, store, large boarding home, and stables. Seven hundred people inhabited the settlement, with 350 of their number employed in the mill. The mechanical equipment of the mill included 10,500 spindles and 424 looms operated by a 500 horse-power engine and three boilers of 600 horsepower capacity.

Robert Ruark fictionalized Delgado Mills in his novel *Poor No More*, calling it Grimes Mills and capturing the atmosphere of the factory and village in which "no intoxicating liquor is permitted to be sold": "A milltown is a milltown.... the filthy skeletons of machinery, the grimy prison aspect of the buildings, the blowing of the whistle, the locking of the gates.... Punch, cut, sew, weave, weld, tread the treadle, swing the crane, check the dial, watch the pump, feed the furnace...." Courtesy of the North Carolina State Archives.

Robert Ruark attended public schools in Wilmington. A journalist and novelist, the author of *Something of Value* and the *Old Man and the Boy* lived on Market Street. In his novel *Poor No More*, Ruark fictionalized Wilmington, saying, "They built it with cotton. Cotton and ships to carry the cotton all over the country." He describes Orton Plantation, calling it Eden and noting "the acres of fallow rice land sweeping toward the river, the forests of blooming magnolia, and acres of exhuberant azalea." Ruark's father, Robert C. Ruark, was Wilmington's postmaster in 1932. Courtesy of the North Carolina Collection, UNC Library, Chapel Hill.

This picture of Peoples Savings Bank on North Front Street at Princess Street was made at 11:30 in the morning of a warm day around 1900. The United Cigar Company across the street from the bank offers forty cents' worth of cigars for a quarter. Peoples Bank was established in July 1873 after being organized in 1872 as the Bank of New Hanover. Its capital was $30,000, with interest paid at four percent per year, compounded quarterly. Bank directors included M. J. Corbett, William Calder, Isaac Bear, and M. W. Divine. Today Wachovia Bank occupies the corner of Front and Market formerly occupied by Peoples Bank. Courtesy of the North Carolina Collection, UNC Library, Chapel Hill.

Two horses make acquaintance just down the street from Fishblate Clothing Company on Front Street at the turn of the century. Farther up the street, the awning of the United Cigar Company protrudes in front of the entrance to the Peoples Savings Bank. Established in 1869 by S.H. Fishblate, the store was located in the Masonic Temple. Mr. Fishblate was mayor of Wilmington for four terms prior to 1900. Courtesy of the North Carolina Collection, UNC Library, Chapel Hill.

The Bijou Theater was the first permanent movie theater in North Carolina and the oldest continuously operated movie theater in the United States. This photograph, made in 1906 when the theater opened, shows owner J. F. Howard with his dog. Admission to the feature was five cents, and "Never Over and Never Out" was owner Howard's theme. Early films viewed by Wilmington patrons were *Black Diamond Express* and *The Great Train Robbery.* The Bijou was closed in 1956. From the Leila W. Miller album.

South Third Street looking north toward Market Street circa 1900. At right is the Hill-Wootten House, built by Dr. John Hill in the early 1800s and torn down in the 1950s when it was sold by the Edward Wootten family to St. James Church next door. The St. James burial ground is directly behind the Hill-Wootten House. Four stories in height, the house had three front porches and fireplaces in each room. A solid mahogany banister rail extended to the third floor, and in the upper hall hung a large brass chandelier with chains designed as vines with clusters of grapes. The entrance porch was paved with slabs of grey slate, and wrought iron grillwork surrounded the porch. Courtesy of James Alfred Miller, Jr.

Leila James Wootten poses on a windowseat before the stained glass windows at the head of the stairs in the Hill-Wootten House at 11 South Third Street. She wears the ruffled dress, sausage curls, and large hair bow characteristic of little girls in 1917. In the old-fashioned flower garden behind the house were lilies of the valley and violets to be picked by the children and worn to Sunday School at St. James Episcopal Church next door. Courtesy of Leila James Garriss.

Beulah Meier, whose downtown dress shop outfitted Wilmington mothers and daughters and career women for many years, waves goodbye in 1915 en route to Hollywood by train to appear in two movies produced by Universal Pictures. Meier is a charter member of the Business and Professional Women's Club of Wilmington and presently makes her home at Wrightsville Beach. Courtesy of Beulah Meier.

The Wilmington Hotel was built on the southeast corner of Front and Walnut streets near the Atlantic Coast Line Railroad depot around 1915. The hotel was erected on property once occupied by the residence of the Borden and Lynch family. The white clapboard home was two stories high, with a front porch which had a view of the Cape Fear River and six bedrooms which caught the river breezes. In this picture of the seven-story brick Wilmington Hotel taken in the early 1900s, the sign on the wall directly across the street advertises Wilmington's prestigious Orton Hotel. Courtesy of the North Carolina Collection, UNC Library, Chapel Hill.

Marchers in a parade follow the trolley car along the cobblestone street at Front and Market near Tom's Drugstore around 1915. From the Julian Martin Collection; courtesy of the Lower Cape Fear Historical Society.

The *Commack* and *Hauppage,* four-masted schooners of 2,200-ton capacity, take shape beneath their scaffolding at the Wilmington Iron Works, pioneer builders of ships of large tonnage. The oldest private business enterprise in Wilmington, the Iron Works was founded in 1838 by Levi Hart and served during the Civil War, the Spanish American War, and World War I. With offices on South Front Street, the firm was known as Hart and Bailey and as Burr and Bailey. A store, machine shop, foundry, copper works, and storage yards made up the business complex. Courtesy of the North Carolina State Archives.

Prior to the completion of the causeway across Eagles' Island in 1924 leading into Wilmington, the ferries *John Knox* and *Menantic* were in constant service on the Cape Fear River. From the Julian Martin Collection; gift of J. J. Fowler; courtesy of the Lower Cape Fear Historical Society.

This is the way the Cape Fear Country Club appeared in 1912 when the Carolina Golf Association held its third annual tournament. Off Oleander Drive, the present club is a large, many-windowed structure with generous porches and many acres of lush golf course. A variety of activities of the annual Wilmington Azalea Festival take place at the Cape Fear Country Club. Gift of Miss Carrie Toomer; courtesy of the Lower Cape Fear Historical Society.

The Champion Independent Football Team of the South included in 1909 Fred Poisson, Bryant Newkirk, George Hashagen, George Parsley, Will Grant, Richard Grant, and W. A. Peschau. Courtesy of the New Hanover County Museum.

The Atlantic Yacht Club was opened in 1895 as the Clarendon Yacht Club at Station Six on the trolley line at Wrightsville Beach. In 1898, the name was changed to the Atlantic Yacht Club, and in 1899 the Big Storm did such damage to the building that it was replaced and a formal re-opening held in June 1900. Commodore James F. Post and members John Bellamy and W.C. Yarborough participated in this event. In 1912, the property changed hands, and the clubhouse was operated as a boarding house by the Misses Herring. Courtesy of the North Carolina Collection, UNC Library, Chapel Hill.

118

An early view of the
Seashore Hotel at the site of
the present Blockade
Runner Hotel. The formal
opening of the Seashore was
held on June 15, 1897. The
cream and white structure
had a veranda 15 feet wide
and 800 feet long which
encircled the main building
as well as 180 rooms and a
pavilion connected by a
boardwalk. Courtesy of the
North Carolina Collection,
UNC Library, Chapel Hill.

The Seashore Hotel Steel
Pier when it opened on July
1, 1910. The first of its kind
on the South Atlantic coast,
it extended 700 feet into the
ocean and was 30 feet wide,
with a two-story pavilion
and observation deck at its
far end. The brightly-lighted
pier was celebrated at a
concert by the Choral
Society of Wilmington in the
pavilion. Performing
members included Albert
Dosher, Mrs. Cameron F.
McRae, and Mrs. Robert C.
Merritt. Courtesy of Lewis
Hall; from *Land of the
Golden River.*

Illegal liquor is destroyed in
front of the Customs House
on Water Street during
Prohibition. North Carolina
had initiated its own
prohibition years before the
national decree by making
liquor illegal in 1909.
Courtesy of the New Hanover
County Public Library.

The Oceanic Hotel at Wrightsville Beach as it appeared in 1925. Named the Tarrymore when it was opened in 1905, the hotel contained 125 rooms facing the sea and had a huge ballroom, bath house and bowling alley. In 1912, two wings were added and the name of the hotel was changed to the Oceanic. It was the center of social activity until it was destroyed in the Big Fire at Wrightsville Beach on January 28, 1934. The fire, which had begun in the Kitty Cottage near Station Two, not only burned the Oceanic Hotel but laid waste the entire north end of the island. Photograph courtesy of the New Hanover County Public Library.

Lumina Pavilion as it appeared in 1905 when it was opened at Wrightsville Beach by the Tidewater Power Company. The "Beautiful Palace of Light" displayed long strings of electric light bulbs outlining the building and was the scene of dancing, athletic events, and other amusements until it was demolished in 1973. Courtesy of the North Carolina State Archives.

Lumina Station, the seventh stop on the electric car line which carried visitors the length of Wrightsville Beach. Courtesy of the *Wilmington Star-News*.

The Fishermen's Dock in front of Oceanic Hotel, Wrightsville Beach, near Wilmington, N. C.

Athletic events were held at Lumina on the Fourth of July, in August, and on Labor Day. Swimming races, canoe races and foot races drew huge crowds. Winners of the foot races in 1912 included George Clark, Isaac Grainger and Charles Jacobs. Photograph courtesy of the New Hanover County Public Library.

Fishermen's Dock in front of the Oceanic Hotel at Wrightsville Beach. The trolley car tracks can be seen at far right leading over Banks Channel from Harbor Island to the beach. James, the seafood vendor, was a familiar sight in the 1930s at Wrightsville, shouting "Swee-ump! Swee-ump!" as he sold shrimp to the summer residents. From a private collection; courtesy of *Scene* magazine.

In 1913, the Tidewater Power Company erected a large movie screen on tall pilings at the edge of the ocean. The projector was housed on the third deck of the Lumina Pavilion, and the 300 seats were arranged in tiers so that spectators could view the movies high above the waves beneath them. Since films were silent at this time, it was an ideal arrangement on a moonlit night. Beneath Lumina Pavilion, among the pilings in the sand, people improvised a "free theater," sitting on boxes and blankets to watch the movie and avoid the price of admission. Courtesy of the New Hanover County Public Library.

The beach car stops at Station One on its run to Wrightsville Beach. Begun in the 1890s, the trollies were operated by Tidewater Power Company until 1939. Each morning at six, the first beach car left the junction of Front and Princess streets in downtown Wilmington and made regular stops every two blocks to Seventeenth Street, where it swung onto what is now Wrightsville Avenue and continued through Delgado and Winter Park to the narrow trestle leading to the beach. After making stops at trolley stations One through Seven, the beach car would make its return run. Lumina Pavilion was built at the end of the trolley line to attract passengers for the beach. Photograph by Cecil Luck; courtesy of B. C. Hedgpeth.

On the east side of the trolley tracks at Station One at Wrightsville Beach was Bud Werkhauser's Stand, an open air structure where cold drinks and newspapers could be purchased. On the west side of the tracks was "Pop Gray's" Soda Shop, the name being derived from a character in a newspaper strip called "Harold Teen." The modern Newell's store evolved from Lester Newell's drink stand and sandwich shop at Station One. Photograph by Cecil Luck; courtesy of B. C. Hedgpeth.

This transfer from the streetcar at Wrightsville Beach was given out during the summer of 1933 to Leila Wootten. A roundtrip ticket from Wilmington to Lumina Pavilion cost 35 cents, with three tickets available for a dollar. Courtesy of Leila James Garriss.

Oyster-gatherers above the trestle leading to Wrightsville Beach do a landslide business in the late 1800s. Two of the most popular oyster roast places were Harrell's on Summer Rest Road and Alex Dock's. Iron salt pans, relics of the Wilmington salt industry, were used to roast the oysters. There is a tradition that oysters can only be eaten in months which contain an "R," which limits the oyster season to September through April. Oysters are usually served with hush puppies and hot pepper vinegar and are best on frosty winter evenings when the steam rises from the opened shells. Oyster shells are used in many of the coastal dwellings as an ingredient of mortar, and they serve as a base for roads leading to the sound. Courtesy of the North Carolina Collection, UNC Library, Chapel Hill.

Admiral Edwin A. Anderson was awarded three Congressional medals of honor for distinguished service in three wars: the Spanish-American War, the occupation of Vera Cruz, and World War I. Admiral Anderson helped quell the Boxer Rebellion in China in 1900, was governor of the island of San Domingo, and commanded the Asiatic fleet. The Anderson home on Masonboro Sound was named Eshcol, meaning a cluster of grapes and chosen because of the scuppernong vines which grew on the property. Courtesy of Crockette Hewlett.

The Walter Parsley residence on Masonboro Sound was designed by Lincoln Memorial architect Henry Bacon in the form of a cross, with octagonal towers and a central rotunda with a circular balcony. The stucco exterior was studded with 30,000 bushels of seashells hauled on flat barges from Masonboro Beach. The distinguished Parsley family had lumber interests in Wilmington. Oscar Grant Parsley, Walter's father, was a director of the Wilmington and Raleigh Railroad and was twice mayor of Wilmington, as well as serving as captain of the Wilmington Light Infantry. Walter Parsley drove around Masonboro Sound in a Packard coupe and was heard to say, "I want to go to heaven when I die, but I had rather live on Masonboro than go to heaven." From the Sue Hall Collection; courtesy of the Lower Cape Fear Historical Society.

George Farrow, in his shop behind his house on Masonboro Sound, was the last of the master boat-builders of the area. Born in 1890, Farrow inherited the trade from his father, John Farrow, who was proprietor of a blacksmith shop on the sound and was the son of Joseph Farrow, the wheelwright. Courtesy of Crockette Hewlett.

Eshcol, the Admiral Anderson house on Masonboro Sound, dated back to 1779. Behind the residence was a tiny dwelling called The Doll's House and built for the admiral's Japanese servant, Sito. In the main house, Admiral Anderson kept bolo knives from the Philippines, machetes from Cuba, guns from the pirate chieftains of China, and embroidered pictures from Japan. Eshcol was torn down in 1963. Courtesy of Crockette Hewlett.

Two members of the Bellamy family, Marguerite Bellamy and Mary Bellamy, flank Elsa Bluethenthal in this picture of the Red Cross workers taken during World War I. From the Sue Hall Collection; courtesy of the Lower Cape Fear Historical Society.

Ships load at the Wilmington wharves in the late 1920s. Courtesy of the New Hanover County Public Library.

THE TWENTIES

Prohibition failed to dampen the spirits of Wilmington citizens during the 1920s. Prosperity kept business and social life at a peak of activity. Wrightsville Beach had become a center of recreation, with Lumina Pavilion, the Seashore Hotel, and the Oceanic Hotel as frequent stops on the trolley car which ran the length of the island. The opening of the causeway to Wrightsville in 1926 made it possible for visitors to go to the popular resort in private automobiles.

In 1927, the plane of Warren Pennington made a landing at the new Wilmington airport, Bluethenthal Airfield, expanding yet another mode of transportation for the New Hanover County area. In 1928, a large sperm whale made an unscheduled landing on Wrightsville Beach at the ocean's edge, bringing townspeople to view the enormous mammal.

The Feast of Pirates, begun in 1927, brought people from all over the state to Wilmington for the celebration built around the buccaneers who had infested the area in the eighteenth century. Merchants dressed their windows, citizens put on costumes, and dramatic and athletic events were held. A band stand was erected in front of the new Cape Fear Hotel, and a street dance was enlivened by the music of the Carolina Aces.

As rum runners brought cargoes of rum and whiskey from the Bahamas and Jamaica, only to be captured by the U. S. Coast Guard in the waters near Wilmington, the young people of the city wore striped blazers, short skirts, and rolled hose, and bobbed their hair. The Crash of 1929 did not immediately affect Wilmington's optimism, for in December the Northeast Cape Fear River Bridge was dedicated and a large procession and grand banquet celebrated the occasion. Visitors to the Port City could continue in their private cars from the mainland into downtown and on to Wrightsville Beach without an interruption in their travel. The tourist trade was a great economic boost to Wilmington, and every effort was made to enhance the area's attractiveness to visitors. Wilmington's fortunate location on the coast helped soften the economic letdown after the high times of the 1920s.

The first Babies Hospital on Wrightsville Sound, with its founder, Dr. J. Buren Sidbury, flanked by the nursing staff. This picture was made in 1920, when the hospital was opened to the public. Dr. Sidbury specialized in the treatment of infants, and in the decades until his death in 1967, he treated thousands of children for ailments ranging from sunburn to critical illness. The proximity of Babies Hospital to the beach, in its location at the entrance to Harbor Island, provided immediate care to those unfortunate children injured in boating or other accidents. Courtesy of the New Hanover County Public Library.

Eliza Wootten was the winner of the $100 first prize in the Baby Parade of 1922. Her ribbon- and gauze-bedecked chariot was drawn through the parade by her sister Leila. Here Eliza stands before her throne wearing her crown and wielding her scepter. Courtesy of Mary Malone Wootten.

Baby parades were popular events at Wrightsville Beach. This one took place in front of the Oceanic Hotel at Station One. Mothers would dress their children in ornate outfits and promenade them in gaily-decorated carriages before the spectators and the judges. Courtesy of the New Hanover County Public Library.

The Coast Guard cutter *Mendota* makes port in Wilmington. The *Mendota* was built between 1928 and 1932. The *Modoc* is another well-known Coast Guard cutter in Wilmington, participating in the Feast of Pirates celebration in 1928. The *Modoc* served on the Greenland Patrol in 1941. Many young men of the Cape Fear area have done service on these vessels. Photograph by Andy Howell; courtesy of the *Wilmington Star-News*.

Uncle Henry Kirkum stands before his oyster roast place prior to his death in 1953. A fisherman, Kirkum started his oyster roast around 1924. He was a familiar sight in his old felt hat and suspenders as he stood with hands in pockets scanning the waters of the sound. In 1954, Hurricane Hazel destroyed this building. Courtesy of Crockette Hewlett.

131

In 1933, Wilmington students were invited to fly at Bluethenthal Airport by the Coastal Plains Airways. Courtesy of Leila James Garriss.

Students' Educational Flight Invitation

THE COASTAL PLAINS AIRWAYS OF WILMINGTON, NORTH CAROLINA, INVITES THE SCHOOL STUDENTS TO FLY AT

BLUETHENTHAL AIRPORT

SATURDAY and SUNDAY, JANUARY 10 and 11

THE PRESENTATION OF THIS INVITATION AND FIFTY CENTS ENTITLES THE SCHOOL STUDENT TO AN AIRPLANE RIDE IN A LICENSED PLANE FLOWN BY A LICENSED PILOT

AN INTERESTING AND EDUCATIONAL AERIAL PROGRAM WILL BE PRESENTED DAILY

In 1927, the first airplane made a landing at the new Wilmington airport, piloted by Warren Pennington. In 1928, the airfield was dedicated and named for World War I hero Arthur Bluethenthal. The airport is now a modern facility known as the New Hanover County Airport. Courtesy of the New Hanover County Public Library.

The causeway to Wrightsville Beach, built by A. E. Fitkin at a cost of $138,000, was opened on June 10, 1926. The ribbon-cutting ceremony took place at four in the afternoon, and a motorcade of 700 automobiles moved over the bridge, signaling the end of the monopoly of the steam trains and trolley cars. Here the ribbons await North Carolina Governor Angus McLean, who did the honors. Photograph from Joe Nesbitt; courtesy of the *Wilmington Star-News*.

Bathing beauty contests were held at Wrightsville Beach in front of the Oceanic Hotel. Here the judges review the contestants, who are clad in the latest-style swimwear. The spectator on the left does not display the same form as the beauties who hold his interest. Winners of the 1927 contest were Grace Rivenbark, Marion Bruff, Mae Murray, and Eunice Taylor. Courtesy of the New Hanover County Public Library.

In April 1928, a sperm whale weighing 50 tons and measuring 54 feet in length washed up at Wrightsville Beach in front of the cottage of M. M. Riley, Jr., an agent of the Clyde Line Steamship Company. Crowds rushed to the north end of the island to view the great mammal until it had lain on the sand for nine days in the hot sun and was no longer attractive. Beach authorities were at a loss to know what to do with the carcass of the whale until curators H.H. Brimley and Harry T. Davis of the North Carolina Museum of Natural History and Resources in Raleigh arranged for it to be brought to the museum as an exhibit. Courtesy of the North Carolina Collection, UNC Library, Chapel Hill.

Motorboat races were held in the late 1920s and early 1930s in Banks Channel at Wrightsville Beach. Races were also held on the Cape Fear River near Wilmington. Courtesy of the New Hanover County Public Library.

Looking east on Princess Street in 1928, an automobile advertises the Feast of Pirates to be held in August. The New York Cafe is always open with a Special 40-cent Dinner, and a nearby restaurant offers chop suey. The astute viewer can distinguish the figure of a man suspended over the street from a trolley cable on the left side of the picture just above the Eureka vacuum cleaners sign. The figure was probably an additional promotion for the Feast of Pirates celebration. Courtesy of the New Hanover County Public Library.

The entrance to the Northeast Cape Fear River Bridge as it appeared in 1929. Visitors entering Wilmington by this route pass over the Cape Fear River, drive past the warehouses at the northern end of the city, and proceed into the downtown district by way of Market Street. Courtesy of the New Hanover County Public Library.

The Northeast Cape Fear River Bridge was dedicated in 1929. Governor O. Max Gardner delivered an address at the city terminus of the bridge, and in the evening there was a great banquet at the Cape Fear Hotel. A large procession made its way through the decorated streets in celebration of the link with the mainland. Courtesy of the New Hanover County Public Library.

View from the Bridge Over the Cape Fear at Wilmington

On a piling in the river
A sea gull sat.
The river flowed around him.
The sun caught the tide's
    surge,
And the bird sat hunched in
    time,
Unmoving as the water
    moved,
As the sunlight moved.
And I—
Watching the gull, the sun,
    and the water—
Stood silent and unmoving.

—From *To the Water's Edge*
by Sam Ragan

The Feast of Pirates was begun in 1927 as an historical pageant which featured pirate scenes on the Cape Fear River and the streets of Wilmington. The August celebration was repeated in 1928 and 1929. Here schoolchildren display their costumes for the event. Local tradition has it that seventeenth century pirate Captain Kidd buried chests of gold coins and silver plate on Money Island at Greenville Sound near Wilmington. The island is several acres in size and is located one mile southwest of Wrightsville Beach. Wilmington children still dig for hidden treasure at this spot. Courtesy of the New Hanover County Public Library.

Red sails in the sunset in Banks Channel off Wrightsville Beach. Sailing regattas were held from the Carolina Yacht Club and the Atlantic Yacht Club, and sailboats of all shapes and sizes could be seen on the waters of the sound and the ocean until the present day. This picture was taken around 1929. Courtesy of the New Hanover County Public Library.

The Greater Wilmington Chamber of Commerce headquarters on Market Street also houses the Greater Wilmington Merchants Association. The restored former residence of William J. Price has been occupied by the Chamber of Commerce since 1968 and is open to visitors who receive information on points of interest in the Cape Fear area. Wilmington's Chamber of Commerce is the oldest in North Carolina, organized in 1866 and merged with the Wilmington Produce Exchange some years after its establishment in 1873. Louis T. Moore is perhaps the best-known secretary of the Chamber of Commerce, gathering and publishing much historical information about Wilmington and photographing many scenes which appear in area collections, including those in this book. Courtesy of the Greater Wilmington Chamber of Commerce.

THE DEPRESSION

Wilmington rallied round during the hard times of the 1930s. The city's population was so interdependent, so tightly woven, that adversity served to stimulate creative solutions to problems and to bring out the cooperative spirit as family members, neighbors, city government, and business people worked together. Many Wilmingtonians recall the worst of times of the Depression era as the best of times, despite the shortage of funds. While certain members of society crumbled under great stress and took their own lives after they had lost their economic strength, many others made the best use of the wonderful facilities at the nearby beaches and sounds and continued to live a satisfying existence.

The white and black high schools, New Hanover and Williston, graduated classes whose members would go on to fame and fortune. Novelist Robert Ruark was a thirties graduate of NHHS, and newspaper editor Tom Jervay was a graduate of Williston. Artist Claude Howell was an NHHS graduate.

WPA projects developed Greenfield Lake and Gardens, under the direction of Public Works Commissioner J. E. L. Wade, and Community Hospital on South Eleventh Street for the Negro population.

In 1934, a fire whipped by gale winds erupted at Wrightsville Beach and destroyed cottages and hotels, one by one, as it spread northward from the Kitty Cottage, a large boarding house. Every structure on the northern end of the island from Banks Channel to the ocean was gutted, except for a handful of private cottages. Prominent Wilmington citizens lost their summer homes, among them Sam Bear, Hargrove and R. R. Bellamy, C. B. Parmele, R. C. Orrell, Julia Post, Carrie Toomer, and Dr. R. Weathersbee. The Oceanic Hotel and "Pop Gray's" soda shop were destroyed in the flames.

Carolina Beach was spared the effects of fire until 1940. Wilmington residents visited this beach south of town to swim in front of the Carolina Moon Pavilion and to socialize at the Bames Hotel. The amusements and rides were of particular interest, for Wrightsville Beach did not offer as many commercial attractions.

Lavish weddings, extravagant debutante parties, teas, luncheons, formal dances, and other entertainments took place throughout the period of the 1930s. While families became resourceful in order to survive the difficult years, some college students temporarily dropping out of school, and automobiles being maintained with special care in order to last a while longer, frugality existed side by side with Wilmington's traditional joy of living. In 1939, many Wilmingtonians attended the New York World's Fair.

Even during the Depression, the Wilmington Chamber of Commerce made every effort to encourage tourism. Although the economic situation severely cut back on travel, these signs welcomed motorists to the "Fine Streets and Suburban Roads" of Wilmington and New Hanover County and invited people to "come again." The speed limit in those days was regulated "by Your Good Judgement and Cooperation." Courtesy of the New Hanover County Public Library.

Local historian and photographer Louis Moore (left) allowed himself to be photographed beside an Atlas tire display at the Esso station on Third Street around 1930. The son of Colonel Roger Moore and Susan Eugenia Beery, Moore worked as a journalist covering the Wilmington waterfront and police courts for several years before becoming secretary of the Wilmington Chamber of Commerce. His historical interests led him to become a charter member of the North Carolina Society of County and Local Historians and a founder of the Lower Cape Fear Historical Society. Moore's book, *Stories Old and New of the Cape Fear Region*, and his panoramic photographs have contributed greatly to the body of knowledge of Wilmington. Courtesy of the New Hanover County Public Library.

The men on relief are paid off on Christmas Eve 1931 in this picture made behind the Post Office in Wilmington. Courtesy of the New Hanover County Public Library.

141

The City Market on South
Front Street was in sun and
shadow during the
Depression. Courtesy of the
New Hanover County Public
Library.

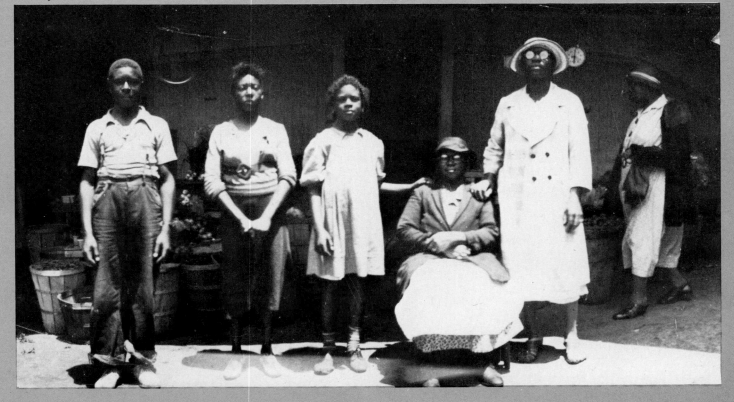

Boat-watching was a favorite pastime on Water Street in Wilmington during the 1930s. Courtesy of the New Hanover County Public Library.

Domestics often took home the laundry of their employers and "did it up," washing and ironing the bed linens and wearing apparel. This woman stirs her wash in the steaming cauldron after scrubbing it in the tub with the aid of a washboard, circa 1930. Courtesy of the New Hanover County Public Library.

A washwoman proudly pushes a baby carriage filled with clean laundry across South Seventh Street in front of Ebenezer Baptist Church in the late 1920s. Courtesy of the New Hanover County Public Library.

Home gardens took on new importance in Wilmington during the Depression. Courtesy of the New Hanover County Public Library.

A Wilmington citizen proudly displays bananas grown in the greenhouse beside his residence in the late 1920s. Courtesy of the New Hanover County Public Library.

Hunters display their antlered booty and prize dogs in front of City Hall and Thalian Hall in the 1930s. Courtesy of the New Hanover County Public Library.

While other Wilmington citizens rode the streetcars, these Depression-era boys used a goat-cart for transportation near the terminus of the street railway. Courtesy of the New Hanover County Public Library.

A bicycle parade in Wilmington in the early 1930s. The Depression returned the bicycle to prominence reminiscent of its halcyon days in the 1890s. Market Street was a popular cycling path at that time, and bicycle clubs such as the Century, the Trio and the University Club erected clubhouses at Hilton Park and the Wilmington and Coast Turnpike near what is now Winter Park. Courtesy of the New Hanover County Public Library.

Maypole dancers celebrate at Robert Strange Park at Eighth and Ann streets around 1930. Courtesy of the New Hanover County Public Library.

A blind man sits in front of
a downtown seafood store
which advertises trout,
blues, flounder, spots,
oysters, clams, mullets, and
shrimp. Despite the
Depression, the fishing was
fine. One of the best-known
seafood businesses was that
of W. H. Yopp, located next to
the City Market. Using his
own boats and nets, Yopp
supplied local patrons and
shipped to Baltimore,
Philadelphia, Washington,
Norfolk, and Richmond. He
owned a city block from
Front Street to the Cape
Fear River, including fish
houses, a restaurant, a dry
goods store, a green grocery,
a barber shop, and a
confectionery business.
Courtesy of the New Hanover
County Public Library.

This blind man carrying a basket and this woman with a basket on her head were familiar sights in Wilmington during the early 1930s, when these pictures were taken. Vegetable vendors came door to door into the 1950s, bringing shelled peas and beans and other produce which could be put immediately into the cookpot and served at the table, greatly reducing the workload of the housewife. Courtesy of the New Hanover County Public Library.

Wilmington's Street Maintenance Department shows off its personnel and its new equipment around 1933. Looking south on Third Street, the vehicles lined up in front of City Hall include trucks, roadscrapers, and rollers. Courtesy of the New Hanover County Public Library.

The 1931 Wilmington Fire Department in the Parade for Progress. Courtesy of the Wilmington Fire Department.

Officials of the Atlantic Coast Line Railroad pose for a picture in the 1930s. George B. Elliott was president of the system in 1930, preceded by R. R. Bridgers, W. G. Elliott, T. M. Emerson, and J. R. Kenly. Courtesy of the *Wilmington Star-News.*

Named after Champion
Davis, president of the
Atlantic Coast Line Railroad,
the Champion was the crack
train of the ACL system.
Courtesy of the New Hanover
County Museum.

The Concourse of the
Atlantic Coast Line Railroad
as it appeared around 1930
from North Front and Red
Cross streets. The ACL
headquarters is on the right.
Courtesy of the New Hanover
County Public Library.

Wilmington and New
Hanover County consoli-
dated their educational
systems in the 1920s, leading the rest of the state in
this effort. New Hanover
High School on Market
Street is shown here as it

appeared in 1932. Novelist
Robert Ruark and newsman
David Brinkley graduated
from NHHS, as did football
stars Sonny Jurgensen and
Roman Gabriel. Courtesy of
the New Hanover County
Public Library.

The faculty of New Hanover High School in 1932 included Principal Dr. W. O. Hampton, Latin teacher Mary Lathrop, art teacher Emma Lossen, mathematics teacher Maie Sanders, and English teacher Martha Stack. These teachers and others taught several generations of Wilmington citizens. Courtesy of Leila James Garriss.

Opposite Page:

This page from the 1932 New Hanover High School Yearbook *Cat Tales* shows the yearbook staff. Editor Elizabeth Whitehead is now married to Julien K. Taylor of Wilmington and has grandchildren of high school age. Assistant editor Nancy Wallace is a published author of children's books and lives in Greenwich Village in New York City. Alfred Miller, business manager, is retired from Bell Telephone Laboratories and teaches business management courses for North Carolina State University; he lives in Morehead City. Courtesy of Leila James Garriss.

THE STAFF
19 32

FRED NEWCOMB
ASSISTANT EDITOR

ELIZABETH WHITEHEAD
EDITOR-IN-CHIEF

NANCY WALLACE
ASSISTANT EDITOR

WOODRUFF CLARK
ADVERTISING MANAGER

ALFRED MILLER
BUSINESS MANAGER

AL DEROO
ASST. ADVERTISING MGR.

DWIGHT McEWEN
ART EDITOR

WILLIAM HOWARD
ASST. BUSINESS MGR.

CHARLES LYNCH
JOKE EDITOR

CORRECTION: Through error, photographs of Al DeRoo and Woodruff Clark were transposed. Al DeRoo is Advertising Manager.—Editor.

19 32

In this picture of the Williston High School Class of 1932, *Wilmington Journal* editor Tom Jervay stands at far right in the front row, hands in pockets. The class motto was "We learn not for school, but for life." Many educators and physicians were in the Class of 1932, among them Dr. John R. Larkins, Dr. William J. Wheeler, Caravelle Carter (C. C.) Chestnut, and Dr. John W. King. The Williston Alumni Association was founded by members of this class and meets on a regular basis in private houses in Wilmington. Photograph by Herbert Howard.

"Williston's Class of 1932"
Class Motto: "We Learn Not For School, But For Life."

The 1949 championship
football team of Williston
High School was under the
direction of Coach Frank
Robinson, far right. The
school was founded in the
1920s by Professor D. C.
Virgo and is presently a
junior high school.
Photograph by Herbert
Howard.

A graduating class stands
on the steps of Williston
High School around 1930.
Courtesy of the New Hanover
County Public Library.

Caterina Jarboro appeared at the Milano Opera House in Milan, Italy, in 1929, and at Carnegie Hall in 1944. Baptized Katherine Yarborough, she was born in Wilmington in 1903. The daughter of a barber, Jarboro was educated in the Catholic schools of Wilmington and the Gregory Normal School. Courtesy of Tom Jervay.

"Watermelon Joe" Howard sold vegetables from a big pushcart at Wrightsville Beach in the 1930s, calling attention to his produce with the song:

Watermelon Joe
Right at yo' do'
You don't have to go
To the sto' no mo'
I got 'em
You want 'em
You bettah come get 'em
Watermelon
Cantaloupe
Peaches
Corn
Tomatoes
Lettuce
Cucumbers
Butterbeans
Peas.

Photograph and song courtesy of Wilmington photographer Herbert Howard, son of Joseph Howard.

Elizabeth Franks Seafood place has stood for sixty years on the Greenville Loop Road. Franks Seafood would catch, cook, clean, pack, and deliver shellfish to retail and wholesale markets six days a week. Clients which purchased the shrimp, crabmeat, clams, and oysters were the Cape Fear Hotel, the King Neptune Restaurant, the Oceanic Hotel, the Surf Club, the Ocean Terrace Hotel, the Kitty Cottage, the Friendly Cafeteria, and Zora's Seafood Market on Castle Street. Thomas J. Franks helped his wife Elizabeth Ward Franks in the business. Courtesy of Elizabeth Franks.

Elizabeth Franks has received many honors during her long life as a Wilmington businesswoman. A member of the Eastern Star, Mrs. Franks learned the seafood business at Wrightsville Sound from her father, George W. Ward. Born in 1898, the year of the Wilmington race riots, Elizabeth Ward Franks was educated at the Wrightsville Sound School and at Miss Emma Boone's School on Ann Street in Wilmington. She lives in a house surrounded by azaleas next to Franks Seafood House on the Greenville Loop Road. Photograph by Herbert Howard.

During the 1920s and 1930s, many famous big bands played at Lumina ballroom: Guy Lombardo, Tommy Dorsey, Paul Whiteman, Stan Kenton, Kay Kyser. Smaller bands were also organized in Wilmington, among them the Carolina Aces. The Aces were Alvah Stanley, trombone; Orrie Whitlock, tuba; Bill Jarman, trumpet; John Tienken, drums; John Allen, banjo; Silas Sheets, piano; Alfred "Prunes" Powell, saxophone; Bill Hancameron, saxophone; and Frank King, saxophone. Courtesy of Lewis Hall; from *Land of the Golden River.*

The ballroom at Lumina as it appeared in the 1930s. Opera chairs surrounded the dance floor, which was waxed and polished weekly. The ballroom was 50 by 120 feet in area, with a promenade 15 feet wide surrounding the dance floor. On the western side, an orchestra shell with a capacity of twenty musicians was equipped with a sounding board which made the acoustics excellent. The ballroom was lit with fifteen tungsten lights of 200 candle power each. Thousands of people would attend the Lumina dances on one evening, and the admission was free. In this view the orchestra shell is at rear center, and spectators sit on the promenade at far right, watching the Fourth of July dance. Photograph courtesy of the *Wilmington Star-News.*

The admission ticket to a special entertainment at Lumina was provided by the Tidewater Power Company to Leila Wootten on July 18, 1933, so that she might help with preparations for Children's Night. Each Friday night, children under twelve years of age were admitted free, and special events were held, such as a cakewalk. Courtesy of Leila James Garriss.

Tide Water Power Company
LUMINA
Complimentary Admission Ticket
GOOD ONLY ON THIS DATE
7/18 _____ 193 3

Issue to
Leila Wootten

This ticket for admission on account of taking part in special entertainment and good only on date shown.

If any alterations are made or ticket presented by other than one originally issued to it will be taken up and full admission charged.

TIDE WATER POWER COMPANY,
L. D. Latta, Sec.-Treas.

No. 434

Cottages at Wrightsville Beach are left high and dry after one of the big storms. This picture was taken around 1930. Courtesy of the New Hanover County Public Library.

Destructive Fire Rakes Wrightsville

Many Cottage Owners At Beach to Rebuild

103 Buildings Are Leveled, Including Oceanic Hotel, With Loss of $1,000,000

CWA AID CONSIDERED

Few Contracts Already Let; Aldermen Called To Meet Today

By AL G. DICKSON
(Staff Correspondent)

WRIGHTSVILLE BEACH, Jan. 28.—The question of the future of Wrightsville Beach, one of the South's oldest and most popular summer resorts, tonight hangs in the gray smoke from the smoldering ashes of 103 of its hotels, boarding houses and private cottages.

The fact that this afternoon's disaster—damage from which is estimated from $500,000 to $1,000,000 —will mean a turning point in the island's history was admitted by practically all persons familiar with its long development.

It is too early to speak of definite plans of reconstruction, however, but arrangements are underway to start the task of clearing the burned area of chimneys and debris this week.

The prediction that 50 per cent of the people whose summer homes were levelled will rebuild within the near future was made by Luther T. Rogers, who has supervised the construction of many a beach house in recent years. His estimate of the damage was $725,- 000.

Returning to his home in Wilmington early in the evening after watching the wind-driven flames sweep the northern part of the strand, Mayor J. A. Taylor announced that a meeting of the board of aldermen will be held tomorrow, probably about noon, to "appraise the situation."

He added that the board will probably appeal to Mrs. Thomas O'Berry, state CWA administrator for permission to assign an emergency force to clean up the burned area in preparation for reconstruction. Mr. Taylor is head of the county CWA division.

"While, of course it is a great disaster, it comes at a time when (Continued on page 3, Column

Detailed Check Places Fire Loss at $728,510

Loss in yesterday's disastrous fire at Wrightsville Beach was estimated at $718,510 by Luther Rogers, local contractor. In addition to this damage to equipment of the Tide Water Power company and the Southern Bell Telephone company was estimated at $5,000 each by officials of those companies.

List of property owners whose homes were destroyed, as compiled by Mr. Rogers, follows:

Carl Dunn; Sam Bear, Sr. and Sons, four houses; E. I. Bear; Mrs. R. R. Bellamy; Hargrove Bellamy, two houses; Belleair Cottage; Mrs. C. B. Bolles; Mrs. Kate Bonitz; W. G. Broadfoot; F. W. Brown; J. L. Bunting; C. E. Beale; T. E. Boyd;

R. C. Cantwell; G. A. Cardwell; Miss Ida Cardwell; Mrs. Jennie Napier, two buildings (Carolina Cottage); John Carter, George Clark.

Miss Nellie Durham; the Mary C. Davis estate; J. E. Evans; C. B. Parmele, two houses; C. D. French; R. G. Grady; G. Henry Haar; John R. Hanby, two houses; E. T. Hancock, two houses; Miss Catherine Vollers; Phillip Heinsburger; A. A. Hergenrother; A. H. Holmes; H. A. Huggins; L. S. Hummell; J. W. Hughes; B. J. Jacobs; Mrs. F. A. Johnson; Mrs. Julian Jordan.

Ben Kingoff; C. J. Kelloway; F. E. Key; Geo. E. Kidder; Miss Margaret Kingsbury; Mrs. J. A. Snyder (Continued _____ Column 3)

Beach Fire from Plane Gives Semblance of Modern Inferno

By LAMONT SMITH
Staff Correspondent

WRIGHTSVILLE BEACH, Jan. 28.—The dread god of fire tramped over the northern extension of Wrightsville Beach this afternoon and lighted the cottages one by one like so many tapers.

When at last, his saga of destruction done, he folded up his wings and soared away, hundreds of cottages lay in smouldering ruins; at least a third of the popular resort was ashy waste, and scores of year-round residents were destitute.

From the air, the scene of destruction was magnificent in its awesome qualities. The island, tiny from an altitude of several thousand feet, was a strip of fire from which billowed dense clouds of smoke, and which gave

the impression of a string of firecrackers going off in rotation. The fire was an insidious snake that wormed its way with deadly persistency from the handsome Kitty Cottage to the almost extreme end of the beach, leaving naught in its wake but crumbling chimneys and smoking debris.

Over the burning area, the air was nearly a vacuum. The ship plunged and dropped and was kept aloft only by the skilful touch of the pilot who, despite the intense heat which billowed up from the ground, swooped to a few hundred feet of the raging flames and then darted outside for a breath of fresh air before coming back for another glimpse.

Perhaps the most perfect description of the scene would be to (Continued on Page 3, Col. 2)

NORTHERN END BURNS

Wind of Near-Gale Force Pushes Flames Relentlessly in Its Path.

STARTS AT 12:30 P. M.

Razing The Kitty Cottage First, Blaze Spreads Rapidly

By EDWIN T. BRINKLEY

WRIGHTSVILLE BEACH, Jan. 28.—Wrightsville Beach, one of the most outstanding and popular summer resorts along the Southeastern coast, was devastated by fire this afternoon.

Starting at 12:30 o'clock in the spacious Kitty cottage, a summer boarding house, the fire swept the entire northern extension of the beach within two and one half hours, causing a property loss reasonably estimated at $1,000,000.

The fire, at first whipped by a brisk westerly wind, enveloped the Kitty cottage and then lashed by a gale that shifted to the southsouthwest, spread to the historic Oceanic hotel, a rambling structure of several hundred joins, and then leaped back to consume the handsome Sprunt, Bear, Wright, and Sternberger summer homes which separated the Kitty Cottage and Oceanic hotel.

Aided by the southwestern blow the flames roared down the northern extension of the resort to consume a total of more than 103 private cottages and boarding houses, leaving only lonesome chimneys in their wake as reminders of what was once the most thickly section of the North Carolina resort.

Only Embers Remain

Wrightsville Beach as it appeared around 1930. Station One is at lower right, with trolley tracks extending southward along what is now South Lumina Avenue. Originally known as New Hanover Banks or Ocean View, the beach was anticipated by its developers to become the "Atlantic City of the South." This was an ambitious undertaking, for in 1897 a meeting of the beach property owners suggested an ordinance to keep cattle from running at large.

Wrightsville Beach has developed from a barely accessible strip of sand to a popular resort with modern condominiums and luxurious private houses. The summer residence of Wilmington citizens for generations, Wrightsville Beach is known not as a commercial district such as Atlantic City, but as a family vacation retreat whose special qualities must be protected from encroachment. Courtesy of the New Hanover County Public Library.

Opposite Page:
The Carolina Moon Pavilion at Carolina Beach was a popular gathering spot until it burned in the fire of 1940. The crowds of Wilmingtonians who visited the beach utilized the bathhouse beneath the large, rambling pavilion and swam in the surf which had no undertow. The Sedgeley Hall Club and the Hanover Seaside Club were established at the beach in 1898 and boasted large memberships. Fishing, boating, amusements and rides continue to attract many visitors. Courtesy of the New Hanover County Public Library.

Carolina Beach as it appeared in the early 1930s. The Bames Hotel, at right behind the National Bread Company truck, was destroyed in the great fire of September 19, 1940, which burned out twenty-four businesses and three entire blocks, including the main boardwalks and the amusement area. Ten miles below Wilmington and Wrightsville Beach, Carolina Beach was attractive to Wilmington citizens because of its commercial area and good fishing waters. Courtesy of the New Hanover County Public Library.

165

During the Depression, WPA workers helped to develop Greenfield Park, digging drainage ditches and creating five-mile-long Community Drive around the lake. The scenic path is a manifestation of the cooperation of Wilmington's citizens to help each other in a time of need and to build something of lasting beauty for succeeding generations. Courtesy of the New Hanover County Public Library.

The *Show Boat* plies the waterways of Greenfield Lake and Gardens, passing among the huge cypress trees and beneath the Spanish moss. Originally called Greenfields and McIlhenny's Mill Pond, Greenfield Park was purchased by the city of Wilmington from the McIlhenny family in 1928, after they had acquired it from Dr. Samuel Green's family. Carl Rehder, founder of the Wilmington School Garden Contests, and the North Carolina Sorosis under the presidency of Mrs. R. W. Hicks, were ardent advocates of the park. City Commissioner James E. L. "Hi Buddy" Wade directed the development of the park in his capacity as head of the Department of Public Works. The rare carnivorous plant Venus Fly Trap grows at Greenfield in a sunken garden. Courtesy of the *Wilmington Star-News.*

Wilmington's Armond W. Scott, appointed by President Franklin Roosevelt as judge of the Municipal Court of the District of Columbia, is greeted by family and friends as he disembarks from the train at the Atlantic Coast Line Concourse. The Scott family lived at Sixth and Walnut Streets, and has produced a veterinarian, a physician, a tailor, a printer, a grocer, a mortician, and a judge, all active members of Wilmington's black community. Courtesy of Scott family archives.

167

The first Community Hospital was established in 1920 on North Seventh Street. Dr. Foster Burnett was a founder of this medical facility for the black community in Wilmington. The first medical clinic in Wilmington was opened in 1949 by Dr. Hubert Eaton, who practices medicine today with his son, Dr. Hubert Eaton, Jr., at the clinic on North Seventh Street near the site of the old Community Hospital. Courtesy of Dr. Hubert Eaton.

Dr. Daniel C. Roane was the first resident physician at Community Hospital. Courtesy of Dr. Hubert Eaton.

Community Hospital on South Eleventh Street was built in 1938 as a WPA project for the black community of Wilmington, replacing the old Community Hospital on Seventh Street. One of the names proposed for the new hospital was the Shober-Mask Hospital, after Dr. James S. Shober, the first Negro physician in North Carolina, and Dr. T. R. Mask. Dr. Shober's office was at 713 Princess Street. In 1967, New Hanover Memorial Hospital replaced Community Hospital and combined the medical facilities for the black and white communities in Wilmington. Courtesy of Dr. Hubert Eaton.

The nursing staff of
Community Hospital on
South Eleventh Street poses
at the entrance to the
hospital in 1950. The first
black registered nurse in
Wilmington was Leonara
Hargrave. Courtesy of Dr.
Hubert Eaton.

Dr. and Mrs. Frank Avant
relax on the beach at
Seabreeze below Wilmington.
Dr. Avant, a Wilmington
physician, and Mrs. Avant, a
nurse, made excursions to
the black resort area on
Sundays in the summer. Dr.
Avant was the president of
the first black medical
society, founded in 1920,
and helped to establish
Community Hospital.
Photograph by Herbert
Howard.

Katherine Meier Baird Cameron, daughter of Beulah Meier, was a favorite model of Wilmington area photographers. A picture of Katherine Meier in a bathing suit fishing at Wrightsville Beach appeared across the top of the North Carolina exhibit at the New York World's Fair in 1939. Courtesy of Beulah Meier.

Wilmington citizens swim in Greenfield Lake during the Depression. The lake and surrounding park often took on a carnival atmosphere, with amusements and rides and sporting events. Courtesy of the New Hanover County Public Library.

Thousands of workers came to the Wilmington Ship Yards during World War II to participate in the building of ships delivered at a record low cost of 403,400 worker hours and $1,543,600. Workers such as those in this picture were sheltered in nearby housing projects hastily erected.

Wilmington mathematics professor Adrian D. Hurst was employed seven days a week at the yards during the crisis. He built his home on Masonboro Sound out of the wooden forms used to construct the huge ships. To prepare the heart pine forms for homebuilding, Hurst employed the services of German prisoners of war who had been contracted out by the U.S. government to a local dairy farmer of Dutch descent.

The POWs pulled the nails and bolts from the used lumber, after first devising a sundial for themselves on Hurst's property so that they could tell the time. Working without an armed guard, the POWs spoke no English but seemed appreciative of the opportunity to associate with American civilians. Solidly built, the Hurst home stands today overlooking the sound in the midst of pines and live oak trees, a monument to the labor of the Germans pressed into constructive activity during a time of war. Courtesy of the New Hanover County Museum.

THE FORTIES

In 1939, the last trolley car made its last trip through the streets of Wilmington, and in 1940, the last beach car ran to Wrightsville. The population of the city was 33,407. World War II brought activity reminiscent of the Civil War and the years of blockade-running. The streets of Wilmington were filled with the activities of the 21,000 workers employed at the North Carolina Shipbuilding Company, and the Cape Fear River was the scene of vessels being constructed for the war effort. Wilmington's young men went off to fight in the military service, and the young women participated in the war effort at home and abroad.

Two new housing projects, Lake Forest and Maffitt Village, quickly went up near the shipyards. In the older residences in town, families were engaged in bidding farewell to sons who had put on military uniforms and welcoming sons who came home on furlough in uniform. Occasionally, telegrams arrived which brought mourning to the households. The newspapers were eagerly read, and radios were listened to with regularity.

When the war ended, Wilmington College opened in the old Isaac Bear School on Market Street across from New Hanover High School, and returning veterans resumed interrupted education. The first Azalea Festival was organized with Hugh Morton as president and starlet Jacqueline White as queen. The parade offered thirty-one floats for the festival-goers who lined the city streets. The Azalea Festival became Wilmington's most well-attended annual event, with golf tournaments, art exhibitions and public dances to attract visitors.

In 1948, before Wilmington slipped into the quiet fifties, America's first Congresswoman and campaigner for women's rights, Jeanette Rankin, made a visit to the city.

The Liberty Ship *Zebulon B. Vance* was the first ship launched at the North Carolina Shipbuilding Company. Named for the governor of North Carolina from 1862-1865, the ship was launched the day before Pearl Harbor, on December 6, 1941, before a crowd of 15,000. Captain Guy Winfield Hudgins was the ship's first captain. In 1948, it was put in mothballs near Newport News, Virginia.

Cape Fear author Guy Owen wrote in *The Apprenticeship of Joel Jarman*, "There was something heady about working at the shipyards...it was the concerted surge of energy that fascinated him, the secret force that welded them all together, the motley subdued men from the mountains, the arrogant self-assured college men, the quiet Negroes from the sharecroppers' shanties. It buoyed him up to see them scrambling over the huge ships, like ants over a giant carcass. He was, for once, part of a collective experience that was worthy of him." Photograph courtesy of the U.S. Maritime Commission.

The *Richard D. Spaight* is launched on September 11, 1942, at the North Carolina Shipbuilding Company. This Liberty Ship was lost to a German submarine off South Africa, one of 250 ships built here from 1941 to 1945. During both world wars, the Wilmington Ship Yards were scenes of frantic activity. The Carolina Ship Yard was established May 6, 1918, with the task of building 10,000 steel freighters. River approaches were dredged and new houses were erected for the thousands of workers. Concrete ships were built at the Liberty Ship Yard, which was founded on May 9, 1918, with Kirby Smith in charge. After World War II, the Liberty Yard became the resting place for the Liberty Ship mothball fleet. At one time, 427 ships were in storage at Wilmington. Among these were the *Henry Ward Beecher*, the *Joseph E. Johnson*, and the *George E. Pickett.* From Wilmington, the ships could be seen across the Cape Fear River as long lines of gray masts against lines of gray cypress trees, ghostly reminders of the holocaust of war. Courtesy of the *Wilmington Star-News.*

The S.S. *Virginia Dare* is launched from the North Carolina Shipbuilding Company yards during World War II. Courtesy of the North Carolina State Archives.

Maffitt Village and Lake Forest were low-cost housing developments hastily constructed near the Wilmington shipyards during World War II. Courtesy of the New Hanover County Museum.

The Coast Artillery from Camp Davis, U.S. Army post north of Wilmington, celebrates at a dance in 1942. In the center of the picture is Grace Jarrell Russ, a nineteen-year-old Wilmingtonian who worked at Camp Davis. The social event took place at the National Guard Armory on Market Street, and the entertainment for the evening was the vaudeville show from the Royal Theater on Front Street.

Camp Davis was erected during World War II and is now closed. Wilmington's young women found employment in office work at the army post, and servicemen came to dances in Wilmington. The life of Grace Jarrell Russ has come full circle. Nearly forty years after she attended the Camp Davis dance at the Armory, she is the receptionist for the New Hanover County Museum headquartered in this same building. Courtesy of the New Hanover County Museum.

The snows came to Greenfield Park during the Winter of 1942, as they had come to Wilmington in 1899 when four days of blizzard put twelve inches of snow on the ground, and as they came to Wilmington in 1980, when a snowfall deposited nearly that amount. Photograph by Edward Wootten; courtesy of Mary Malone Wootten.

Descendants of Richard Bradley gather at the Carolina Yacht Club in 1944. From a private collection.

The Carolina Yacht Club was founded in 1853 by a group of Wilmingtonians which included Richard Bradley, Daniel Baker, Parker Quince, John Reston, R. J. Jones, Talcott Burr, and T. M. Gardner. In existence 127 years, the club is the second oldest yacht club in America, predated only by the New York Yacht Club.

Located in the center of Wrightsville Beach next to the water tower, the Carolina Yacht Club provides a social atmosphere conducive to family activities and is a gathering place for many generations of Wilmingtonians. Sailing regattas are held frequently, attracting sailors from yacht clubs up and down the east coast.

Memberships in the club are handed down through families. Wilmington merchant Richard Bradley was the first Commodore of the club. His regatta-winning boat was named the *Princess*, with subsequent yachts named the *Hiawatha* and the *Minnehaha*. Courtesy of the North Carolina Collection, UNC Library, Chapel Hill.

The Carolina Yacht Club as it appeared in 1910. Destroyed during Hurricane Hazel in 1954, it was rebuilt the following year. On the upper floor of the main building is a large social room and bar, with a dance floor on the lower level. The two wings house dressing rooms, a nursery, a dining porch, a snack bar, and a kitchen, with a large covered porch encircling the main building and connecting the wings. Until the berm was constructed on Wrightsville Beach, at high tide the ocean would wash up under the Club porch. Courtesy of the North Carolina State Archives.

Prior to the construction of a berm at Wrightsville Beach, jetties were used to control erosion. Extending from the shore far out into the ocean, the tar-coated, barnacle-encrusted jetties were favorite spots for gathering seashells. On moonlit nights, courting couples would go "jetty-jumping." Waves washed over the jetties at high tide, as in this picture taken by Edward Wootten in 1942. Photograph courtesy of Mary Malone Wootten.

The Ocean Terrace Hotel stood on the site occupied by the Blockade Runner Hotel today at Wrightsville Beach. In 1935, the name of the Seashore Hotel was changed to the Ocean Terrace Hotel and for the next twenty years was the scene of bustling summer activity. The large parking lot was filled with automobiles, the long porches with visitors in rocking chairs, and the pavilion at lower right with young people. In 1954, the Ocean Terrace was severely damaged by Hurricane Hazel and burned to the ground in 1956. Courtesy of the Wrightsville Beach *Gazette*.

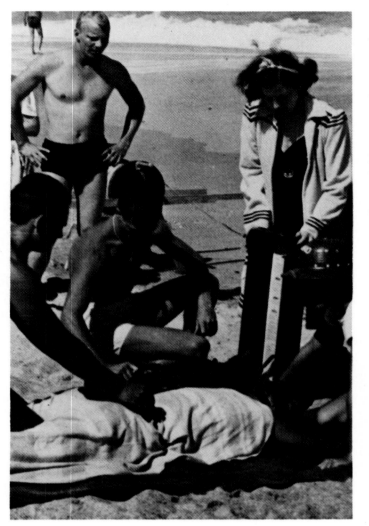

Opposite Page:
This photograph of the Wilmington members of the National Association of Letter Carriers in Wilmington was taken in the 1940s by black photographer Herbert Howard, son of "Watermelon Joe" Howard. Howard began taking group photographs in 1927 and still keeps an active darkroom in his residence on South Thirteenth Street. Courtesy of Herbert Howard.

Hannah Block, Mayor Pro Tem of Wilmington from 1961 to 1965, was the first female lifeguard on the coast of North Carolina. From 1941 to 1949, she patrolled the strand as head lifeguard at Carolina Beach. In this photograph taken in 1945, Hannah Block trains guards in giving first aid during a rescue operation. Photograph courtesy of Hannah Block.

The Seashore Hotel as it existed before 1935. As one of the most exclusive resort hotels on the Atlantic Coast, in 1905 it employed a superb headwaiter named William D. Polite, who also worked at nearby Orton Plantation and was known as Polite the Butler. Dressed in frock coat and starched collar and cuffs, standing perfectly straight, he was a fine drawing card for the hotel. In 1909, he marketed Polite's Pepper Sauce, which he made behind his home on Thirteenth Street in Wilmington. Soon he added Polite's Sea Food and Steak Sauce. In 1926 he founded the Waiters and Cooks Association. Courtesy of the New Hanover County Public Library.

Althea Gibson, 1951 World Tennis Champion at Wimbledon, with Wilmington physician Dr. Hubert Eaton on the tennis court at his Orange Street home in 1948. Gibson came to Wilmington in 1946 from New York City to live as a member of Dr. Eaton's family and attend Williston Senior High School, from which she graduated in 1949. During her three years in Wilmington, Gibson perfected her tennis skills to go on to become the first American Negro to play at Forest Hills.

Dr. Hubert Eaton, Althea Gibson's mentor, is himself a tennis champion, winning the 1934 National Junior Championship of the American Tennis Association, and becoming National Intercollegiate Champion and Doubles Champion of the CIAA. Dr. Eaton is also a pioneer in the civil rights movement, in 1951 and 1963 successfully filing suits against the New Hanover County Board of Education to integrate the schools. Courtesy of Dr. Hubert Eaton.

The Wilmington Fire Department knocks down the walls of the Orton Hotel on Front Street in the fire which destroyed the building in 1949. Courtesy of the Wilmington Fire Department.

New Hanover High School students Sally Hicks, Margaret Head, Anne Miller and Katherine Graham (left to right) grace a float in the 1953 Azalea Festival parade. Courtesy of Leila James Garriss.

Miss Wilmington rides the Atlantic Coast Line float in an Azalea Parade in the late 1940s. The first Azalea Festival was organized in 1948, with Hugh Morton as its president and movie star Jacqueline White as its queen. There were thirty-one floats in the parade. The festival has expanded in the past three decades to include a golf tournament, outdoor art exhibit, and many associated activities, making it the largest annual event in Wilmington. From the Sue Hall Collection; courtesy of the Lower Cape Fear Historical Society.

The riverfront fire of 1953 occurred at the Wilmington Terminal and Warehouse Company on the Cape Fear River at the north end of the city. Explosions of burning nitrates sent up clouds of smoke which could be seen all over Wilmington, and the fire was fanned by a strong north wind. As the Wilmington Fire Department battled the blaze, the U.S. Coast Guard lent its assistance, and volunteer groups such as the Red Cross and the Gray Ladies distributed coffee and doughnuts to the workers. Classes at New Hanover High School were ignored as students left school to go down to view the disaster. Courtesy of the Wilmington Fire Department.

THE FIFTIES

During the 1950s, older Wilmingtonians listened to "Stop the Music" over their radios while the teenagers gathered at the Dixie Pig Nos. One and Two on the beach roads to share milkshakes and hamburgers. The most memorable events of the period were two natural disasters, the fire in 1953 which occurred at the nitrate warehouse on the river at the north end of the city, and Hurricane Hazel, which struck in October 1954. Hazel is remembered to this day for its violence and destructiveness, succeeding storms being measured against this killer storm. Hitting the coast at 140 miles an hour, Hazel left seven million dollars worth of damage in its wake.

Another event which had a lasting effect on the profile of the area was the announcement in 1955 that the Atlantic Coast Line would move its offices from Wilmington. The dreaded moment had arrived when Wilmington citizens would be forced to leave jobs which had sustained them for years or to move to other states far away from the people and places they loved. A downcast mood prevailed over the city.

The news was not all bad during these years. In 1952, the first of the State Ports Authority terminals was completed at Wilmington. This new facility would help offset the loss of the Coast Line headquarters. In 1955, the Wilmington Committee of One Hundred was organized to stimulate economic development.

The old Bijou Theater, which had given entertainment to generations of Wilmingtonians, was closed, and the Wilmington Public Library moved into the Armory of the Wilmington Light Brigade Infantry on Market Street. The Korean War took some of the city's young men away to serve in the military and brought still other young men from faraway towns to Wilmington on leave from the nearby marine base, Camp Lejeune. The 1950s closed with a quality of stagnation, many of Wilmington's young people looking to other areas to seek employment and rear families. The hustle and bustle of the Port City had slowed to a meandering walk.

The fire house at the corner of Fourth and Dock streets, shown in this picture, was replaced by the present headquarters in 1955. Firemen practiced in the tower located behind the building. Courtesy of the Wilmington Fire Department.

Agnes Moorehead posed on the steps of Thalian Hall when she appeared at the Wilmington theater on October 28, 1954, in *That Fabulous Redhead*. Other stars who appeared at Thalian Hall during its long history were Otis Skinner, Lillian Russell, Louise Dresser, Ruth St. Denis, and Maude Adams. Courtesy of Thalian Hall.

Hurricane Hazel struck Wilmington on October 15, 1954. The killer storm came in at 140 miles per hour, doing $7 million worth of damage at Wrightsville Beach and destroying or severely damaging 250 buildings there. At the Red Cross relief headquarters in Wilmington at Second and Orange streets, the Reverend Mortimer Glover of St. James Episcopal Church led the disaster team. The storm had a lasting effect on the landscape of Wrightsville Beach, causing oldtimers to date events as Before Hazel or After Hazel. Courtesy of the *Wilmington Star-News*.

The surf rolls in on one of the streets at Wrightsville Beach as Hurricane Hazel approaches its height. All four of the cottages shown in this picture were completely demolished by the storm. Courtesy of Mary Malone Wootten.

Wrightsville Beach shows the aftermath of Hurricane Hazel. The Carolina Yacht Club and the Ocean Terrace Hotel were destroyed, and the Neptune Restaurant was badly damaged. Courtesy of the North Carolina State Archives.

The seven-story headquarters building of the Atlantic Coast Line Railroad at North Front and Red Cross streets was blown up in 1970. In 1960, the Coast Line moved its headquarters from Wilmington to Florida, putting into action a rumor which had circulated since 1900 that the offices would be moved to another city. The loss of the Coast Line headquarters was a severe blow to Wilmington, for many of its citizens earned a living as ACL employees, and the economy of the area was in large part dependent on the Coast Line. Some employees retired and others looked for new lines of work when the Coast Line left. Still others uprooted their families from Wilmington and transferred to Coast Line offices in other cities. Photograph by Andy Howell; courtesy of the *Wilmington Star-News*.

188

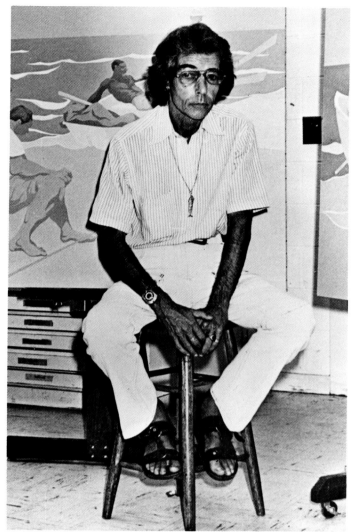

Whimsical Christmas card designed by Claude Howell in 1953. Friends of the artist have collected his original Christmas greetings for many years. This scene depicts the historic Carolina Apartments on Market Street, where Howell makes his home and has his studio. He may be seen decorating his Christmas tree in the third window from the right, third story down. Courtesy of Leila James Garriss.

Claude Howell, Wilmington artist and chairman of the art department at the University of North Carolina at Wilmington until his retirement in 1980, has exhibited at the 1940 New York World's Fair, the North Carolina Museum of Art, and the Metropolitan Museum of Art. Now working out of his studio in the historic Carolina Apartments on Market Street, Howell studied under Wilmington artists Elisabeth Chant and Henry MacMillan. Students of Howell have included Wilmington artists Emma Lossen and Hester Donnelly. Courtesy of the University of North Carolina at Wilmington.

The Kenan Memorial Fountain at the intersection on Fifth and Market streets is a downtown landmark. Designed by architects Carrere and Hastings and installed in 1921, the huge fountain lost one of its bottom tiers in the 1950s when it was removed to enable traffic to flow more smoothly around its base. Courtesy of J. Bradford Wiggins.

The World's Largest Christmas Tree, a venerable oak, is decorated at Hilton Park each holiday season. Former mayor James E. L. "Hi Buddy" Wade turned on the lights during the annual festivities until his death in 1980. Photograph by Hugh Morton; courtesy of *Scene* magazine.

"Hi Buddy" James E. L. Wade waved to a friend as he crossed a downtown street in 1980 shortly before his death in July. A former mayor of Wilmington, state senator, and city council-man, Wade established the first USO offices in Wilming-ton. Known as "Santa Claus" and "Daddy Greenfield," Wade helped to create Greenfield Park. When he was over ninety years old, Wade took a daily stroll downtown carrying his Italian black cane with an engraved sterling silver handle. In his heyday, Wade lunched twice with John F. Kennedy, had dinner with Herbert Hoover, and in-structed Eleanor Roosevelt in the proper way to eat Southern fried chicken, with her fingers. He was so well known by so many people that he received his mail at the simple address, "Hi Buddy 28401." Photograph by Jim Erickson; from the Raleigh *News and Observer*.

All-America quarterback Roman Gabriel, star of the North Carolina State University Wolfpack and the Los Angeles Rams, was born in Wilmington August 5, 1940. The son of Filipino immigrant R. I. Gabriel, the 6'4" athlete excelled at football, basketball, and baseball at New Hanover High School under Coach Leon Brogden. Gabriel was voted Most Valuable Player in the National Football League in 1969. Courtesy of North Carolina State University.

Sonny Jurgensen, quarterback for the Washington Redskins, is a native of Wilmington. Named Best Passer in the National Football League, Jurgensen played football at New Hanover High School in the early fifties under Coach Leon Brogden. Courtesy of the North Carolina State Archives.

The U.S.S. *North Carolina* comes to Wilmington in October 1961, guided up the Cape Fear River to her resting place at Eagles Island. The battleship was the pride of the United States Navy, fighting in every major engagement in the Pacific theater in World War II. Her overall length is 728 feet, 9 inches, with an extreme beam of 108 feet, 4 inches, and a standard displacement of 35,000 tons. Carrying 108 officers and 1,772 enlisted personnel, she has a designed speed of 27 knots, and her armament includes nine 16-inch guns. A major tourist attraction, the U.S.S. *North Carolina* Battleship Memorial has had over four million visitors. Photograph by Hugh Morton; courtesy of the *Wilmington Star-News*.

THE SIXTIES

The 1960s opened with vigor. The battleship *North Carolina* arrived in October 1961 and was maneuvered into her final mooring at Eagles Island, restored to become a significant tourist attraction for Wilmington. Urban renewal was approved, and necessary demolition of unsightly structures was undertaken. Unfortunately, the early zeal of urban renewal also took down historic homes which would have been restored had they lasted until the 1970s.

Educational facilities expanded. Construction on Cape Fear Technical Institute was begun in 1965, and in 1968 Wilmington College became part of the university system. The University of North Carolina at Wilmington, as it is now known, sits on a large campus with many new buildings.

Construction of New Hanover Memorial Hospital, which would replace Community Hospital and James Walker Hospital, started in 1965. Not coincidentally, five new industrial plants announced ambitious expansion in Wilmington, DuPont, Corning Glass, Hercules Inc., Filtors Inc., and General Electric. A new hotel on the river, Timme Plaza (Hilton Inn), was built. A new high school, Hoggard, was dedicated. The new Cape Fear Memorial Bridge, begun in 1966, was opened in 1969.

Legal and political activity which would profoundly affect Wilmington was taking place as the 1960s came to an end. The Wilmington school system was ordered to desegregate in 1969, following rioting after the 1968 assassination of the Reverend Martin Luther King. The social fabric began to show strain, even as economic health returned to the city.

This early evening photograph of the United States Customs House on Water Street was taken in the 1960s. The Coast Guard cutter *Mendota* and Fergus' Ark restaurant are docked in the Cape Fear River in front of the government building. The Customs House was built in 1916 as a result of efforts by B.F. Keith and Colonel Walker Taylor, collectors of customs. Courtesy of the North Carolina Collection, UNC Library, Chapel Hill.

The Vought OS2U Kingfisher, integral aircraft for the U.S.S. *North Carolina*, used the radio call sign "Showboat, this is Sitting Duck." The Kingfisher, which was launched by catapult from the stern of the battleship, participated in the rescue of many United States pilots shot down by Japanese anti-aircraft. This Kingfisher was lost in dense fog on a flight to Alaska in 1942 and was discovered twenty-two years later on Calvert Island 300 miles north of Vancouver, British Columbia. Restored to its original condition, the Kingfisher was brought to the deck of the U.S.S. *North Carolina* in 1971. Courtesy of *Scene* magazine.

Charlie the alligator makes his home in the Cape Fear River near the U.S.S. *North Carolina* Battleship Memorial, to the delight of schoolchildren visiting "The Immortal Showboat." Charlie is just one of several alligators who can be seen sunning themselves or poking their snouts up out of the river. Alligator-hunting was a favorite pastime of young people in the 1930s as they made excursions by boat through the marshes surrounding Wilmington. Photograph by Hugh Morton; courtesy of the *Wilmington Star-News.*

The city of Wilmington's fireboat, the *Atlantic IV*, in full operation at the rate of 2,500 gallons per minute. With its crew of four, the steel-hulled vessel has protected warehouses, piers and ships on the Cape Fear River for the two decades since it was built in 1932 as a Navy patrol boat. One of its first duties in 1961 was to wash down the decks of the U.S.S. *North Carolina* before dedication of the battleship as a war memorial. Fireboats *Atlantic I,* serving between 1907 and 1914, *Atlantic II* until 1948, and *Atlantic III* until 1961 were of wooden construction. Courtesy of the *Wilmington Star-News.*

During his term as governor, Bob Scott officially dedicated the University of North Carolina at Wilmington. Courtesy of the *Wilmington Star-News.*

195

The University of North Carolina at Wilmington offers bachelor's degrees in the liberal arts, sciences, fine arts, and technologies as well as graduate programs in education and business administration. Because of its location on the coast, the university offers a popular course in marine archaeology and is the choice of many out-of-state students who wish to attend school by the sea. Courtesy of the University of North Carolina at Wilmington.

A turn-of-the-century soiree at Isaac Bear School on Market Street saw the school gaily decorated and horse-drawn carriages lining the street. The occasion may have been the visit of President William Taft to Wilmington in 1909. Isaac Bear School became Wilmington College in 1947. From a private collection; courtesy of *Scene* magazine.

Wilmington College was founded in 1947 on Market Street not far from New Hanover High School in the old Isaac Bear School, as shown in this photograph. Sponsored by the city of Wilmington, the college utilized the services of many Wilmingtonians, among them mathematics professor Adrian Hurst and artist Claude Howell. The college became a part of the North Carolina university system in 1968 and is now the University of North Carolina at Wilmington, located in a sprawling complex of new buildings on the College Road campus. Courtesy of the Greater Wilmington Merchants Association.

Opposite page:
Rebuilt in 1979, the Northeast Cape Fear River Bridge opens to allow a ship to pass upriver. Beyond the warehouses at the top of the picture, the buildings of downtown Wilmington may be seen. Photograph by Hugh Morton; courtesy of the *Wilmington Star-News.*

Cape Fear Technical Institute is a downtown educational institution on North Front Street which offers one- and two-year degree programs and has a strong emphasis on the sea. Its campus includes a pier used by ocean research vessels which are part of the marine instruction program. Courtesy of the *Wilmington Star-News*.

The ten-story New Hanover Memorial Hospital on South Seventeenth Street marked a turning point in Wilmington's history. Opened in 1967, the new hospital employs over 1,600 persons and substantially affects the economy of the area. An active, bustling city, after World War II Wilmington slipped into economic stagnation in the quiet 1950s, to come back to life in the late 1960s when physicians and business interests saw the contemporary medical facility become a reality. New Hanover Memorial Hospital replaced James Walker Hospital and Community Hospital. Photograph by Robert McClure, Jr.; courtesy of New Hanover Memorial Hospital.

Lying between the Cape Fear River and the Atlantic Ocean, Wilmington is a city of bridges. Here a ship passes under the Cape Fear Memorial Bridge, dedicated in 1969. Looking upriver, the buildings of the city are on the right. The highway over the bridge leads east toward Wrightsville Beach. Photograph by Hugh Morton; courtesy of the *Wilmington Star-News*.

This recent photograph of Wilmington captures both the new and the old flavor of the city. Contemporary buildings mingle with historic homes as the spires of venerable churches rise above the tree-tops. The log boat *Edward M*, excursion boat *J. N. Maffitt*, schooner *Harry W. Adams*, and tugboat *John Taxis* are docked in the Cape Fear River at Chandler's Wharf, making time stand still for the viewer who might imagine it is the turn of the century until the late-model automobiles parked beside the river come into focus. Photograph by Roy Zalesky; courtesy of the Greater Wilmington Chamber of Commerce.

Mike's Grill and Grocery Store at Sixth and Ann streets was fire-bombed in 1971 as a pivotal episode in a period of racial violence which resulted in the conviction of The Wilmington Ten, led by the Reverend Ben Chavis. A National Guardsman stands at the door of Gregory Congregational Church after federal troops were called to Wilmington during the 1971 riots. Racial tensions had built in the city following the closing of Williston High School and the transferring of students and teachers to New Hanover High School. Hoggard High School had been opened by this time. Students involved in the racial incidents met in Gregory Congregational Church. Courtesy of Tom Jervay.

THE SEVENTIES

In 1971, Wilmington experienced racial conflict similar to that occurring in other cities across the nation. With civil rights consciousness raised among Wilmington's young people and frustration at a high level, the black and white communities found themselves at odds during a period of violence. Mike's Grill and Grocery Store was fire-bombed, and the National Guard was called in to quell the disturbance.

In subsequent events, the Wilmington *Journal*, a black newspaper edited by Tom Jervay, was also fire-bombed. This period of conflict brought national attention as The Wilmington Ten, led by the Reverend Ben Chavis, were sent to prison and taken on as a cause by civil rights activists. Parallels were made with the 1898 racial riots.

The decade of the 1970s saw the end of the old Lumina Pavilion, which had inspired many happy memories in Wilmington citizens. It was torn down in 1973, as it had become too expensive to maintain. New beginnings were made through efforts of the Historic Wilmington Foundation and the Downtown Area Revitalization Effort.

The new seven-story hospital with its adjacent medical support services, the new Independence Mall on Oleander Drive, the new industries, and the restoration of the downtown area have attracted many new residents to the city and brought home many former residents. Wilmington today combines the best of the new and the old, with gracious homes once again showing elegant facades, contemporary structures giving a look of progress, established families providing a strong foundation, and recently arrived families bringing fresh ideas. Having endured many crises and become stronger through cooperative effort, Wilmington enters the 1980s as a vital port city of diverse resources and interests.

The distinctive areas of Wilmington, the river, the sounds, the beaches, the business district, the residential suburbs, the shopping malls, the agricultural lands, and the industrial sections work together to provide a stimulating overall environment. The two disparate groups, the conservators and the innovators, both lend their energies to create a mix of heritage and progress which keeps the city interesting to live in and to visit. As old marble fireplaces are refurbished, new solar homes are being designed. The highway from Wilmington toward Raleigh is widened and improved. Wilmington cherishes its past and looks to its future, confident that its unique combination of natural resources will carry it forward into its next exciting decade.

Free the Wilmington Ten Rallies took place after the conviction of the Reverend Ben Chavis and nine of his colleagues for participation in the 1971 Wilmington race riots. This rally took place in the North Carolina state capital, Raleigh. Courtesy of Tom Jervay.

Tom Jervay (left), editor of the *Wilmington Journal*, sits with Wilmington native David Brinkley of NBC News and Southern Pines journalist Sam Ragan (center), who was City Editor of the *Wilmington Star-News* papers in the 1940s. Jervay is the senior black editor in North Carolina and has been president of the National Newspaper Publishers Association. He began his career as a shop devil in his father's printing company, which was located in the same building as the newspaper. The *Wilmington Journal* was established in 1927 as the *Cape Fear Journal* and currently has a weekly circulation of 8,000. Until 1970, the Jervay family lived upstairs over the newspaper offices. Courtesy of Tom Jervay.

The *Wilmington Journal* offices on South Seventh Street were fire-bombed in the early 1970s by a member of the Rights of White People organization. Extensive repairs were made to the building. Courtesy of Tom Jervay.

A feature of the annual Azalea Festival in Wilmington is the sidewalk art show. This one took place in 1974 on Orange Street next to the Community Art Center. The Lower Cape Fear Council on the Arts and the Wilmington Parks and Recreation Department are housed in this former USO building built during World War II using a standard plan. Erected in haste and intended to be temporary, the USO on Orange Street has withstood the years and continues to be a focal point for cultural activities in Wilmington. From *Two Centuries of Art in New Hanover County*; courtesy of Crockette Hewlett.

Meadowlark Lemon embraces young Wilmington fans during a 1971 visit to his hometown when he was the comedy star of the Harlem Globetrotters. Meadow George Lemon III first played basketball at the Community Boys' Club and later at Williston Senior High School under Coach Frank Robinson and Coach E. A. "Spike" Corbin. Operating his own basketball club since leaving the Globetrotters, the "Clown Prince of Basketball" has performed in over 100 countries, endearing himself to millions of people throughout the world and promoting better understanding between the races. Photograph by Hugh Morton; courtesy of Tom Jervay.

Independence Mall was opened on August 1, 1979, off Oleander Drive. The huge shopping complex houses major department stores such as Belk-Beery, J. C. Penney, and Sears, and a wide variety of specialty stores which attract Wilmington citizens and contribute to the economy of the area. Courtesy of Hoggard High School.

The Boys' Club on Nixon Street near D. C. Virgo School was torn down in 1979. Originally built by the United States government as a USO during World War II, the Boys' Club was a favorite haunt of basketball star Meadowlark Lemon when he was growing up in Wilmington. Photograph by Herbert Howard.

CBS newsman Charles Kuralt was born in Wilmington during the Depression. Spending his boyhood on his grand-father's two-mule, one-cow tobacco farm in Cape Fear country near Stedman, at age eight he mimeographed his own neighborhood gazette. At age fourteen, his broadcasting career began when North Carolinian Edward R. Murrow read his winning essay for the "Voice of Democracy" contest over CBS radio. Editing the *Daily Tar Heel* at the University of North Carolina at Chapel Hill, reporting for the *Charlotte News*, and broadcasting "On the Road" and "Sunday Morning" on television followed. Photograph by Robert Philips; courtesy of *Quest/81* magazine.

Wilmington native Charles Everette "Hoss" Ellington, racecar driver. Photograph by Roy Zalesky; courtesy of *Scene* magazine.

Ida Brooks Kellam, Wilmington historian. An incorporator of the Lower Cape Fear Historical Society, Mrs. Kellam was awarded the Ruth Coltrane Cannon Cup in 1971 "for her careful and valuable research along numerous lines of historical importance." She taught for thirty years in the Wilmington public schools. Courtesy of the *Wrightsville Beach Gazette*.

Opposite Page:

David Brinkley, shown relaxing at Chandler's Wharf in 1976, graduated from New Hanover High School. The NBC newscaster worked in the summer at the Lumina concession stand and later at the *Wilmington Star-News*. Photograph by Roy Zalesky; courtesy of *Scene* magazine.

A three million dollar container crane at the State Port Terminal in Wilmington, with its sister crane in the background. The cranes service some 900 international vessels each year. Photograph by Roy Zalesky; courtesy of the State Ports Authority.

David Brinkley's birthplace on the corner of Eighth and Princess streets is no longer standing. Courtesy of the *Wilmington Star-News*.

204

Tom Wright, Wilmington preservationist who created Chandler's Wharf on the banks of the Cape Fear River and spearheaded restoration of the historic district, stands before the deRosset House at the corner of Second and Dock streets. Built by Dr. Armand John deRosset in 1841, the house is an example of Italianate architecture and is being restored to its former elegance by the Historic Wilmington Foundation. The revitalization effort for the downtown business district is called DARE. Photograph by Roy Zalesky; courtesy of *Scene* magazine.

Chandler's Wharf is a reconstruction of the nineteenth century era of sailing schooners and paddle-wheel steamboats. At the south end of Water Street off Ann Street, the complex includes six historic vessels, a harbor master's house built in 1853, an iron works building built in 1889, a nautical museum, and a waterfront restaurant in the restored home of Wilmington merchant William E. Craig, who operated a cooperage until 1883. Courtesy of the *Wilmington Star-News.*

The Cotton Exchange occupies a site on Front Street where Alexander Sprunt & Son operated one of the largest cotton export companies in the world in the late 1800s. A complex of shops and restaurants, the Cotton Exchange rises four stories above the Cape Fear River and is a maze of narrow walkways and stairways which lead to art galleries, book shops, jewelry stores, and many other commercial enterprises in restored buildings such as that of the Boney-Harper Milling Company, which manufactured corn grits in 1884. Photograph by Carl Seibert; courtesy of the *Wilmington Star-News*.

Aerial photograph of the State Port Terminal at Wilmington in 1980, showing 6,040 feet of continuous concrete wharf and 1,132,582 square feet of warehouse space, and two 40 long-ton container cranes. The channel is 38 feet at mean low water. Courtesy of the North Carolina State Ports Authority.

This aerial view shows Wilmington as it appears today looking eastward across the Cape Fear River toward Wrightsville Beach ten miles away. In the foreground is Eagle Island with the U.S.S. *North Carolina* at berth. A Coast Guard vessel, the *Northwind*, is docked just upriver from the Customs House, and the fireboat *Atlantic IV* is at the foot of Market Street at the southern end of the Customs House.

Farther up Market Street, on the right side, are the Burgwin-Wright House and St. James Episcopal Church on the corners of South Third Street. Behind these are the Temple Israel and the Carolina Apartments, at Fourth and Fifth streets. On the left side of the photograph, the modern Hilton Inn rises up beside the river, and behind it is the Cotton Exchange. Princess, Chestnut, Grace, and Walnut Streets parallel Market Street running east from the river. Photograph by Jerry Blow of Penumbra.

By the 1980s Wilmington was on a roll. Designated in 1983 by the North Carolina General Assembly as the state's first international city, Wilmington attracted flamboyant Italian filmmaker Dino de Laurentiis, who brought a major movie production studio to town. Soon big film stars such as Richard Gere and Sissy Spacek were sunning on the beaches and rubbing elbows with locals in downtown restaurants. The venerable Carolina Apartments, busy Front Street, lush Airlie Gardens, and beloved New Hanover High School were among many features of the Port City landscape transformed into scenes in big-budget movies showing in theaters across the country. Residents saw themselves on the wide screen as extras or in speaking roles, and some found new careers as film technicians.

Wilmington citizens made an official excursion abroad to establish a sister-city relationship with Dandong, China, and to create new trade opportunities. The Marine Crescent was established to promote ocean-related research. A multi-million dollar airport terminal was under way, with a 247-acre industrial park. A segment of I-40 was completed to connect Wilmington with the coast-to-coast highway. The Japanese-owned Takeda Chemical Products USA selected Wilmington for a vitamin B-1 plant in 1986 and a $95 million vitamin C plant in 1989, and the city became the fastest-growing retail and service market in the state.

A Convention and Visitors Bureau was opened in the historic courthouse downtown. Grand old Thalian Hall was made even grander with a major renovation and addition, and St. John's Museum of Art restored the original lodge while expanding gallery space. The new Coast Line Convention Center opened on the riverfront. Dozens of entrepreneurs established themselves in the downtown commercial district, and the old Manor Theater on Market Street was transformed into the trend-setting Jacob's Run entertainment complex, offering hot bands, new plays, foreign films, and upscale dining. Front Street News became a gathering place for the community's intellectuals and artists. And Wilmington's own Michael Jordan emerged a national basket-

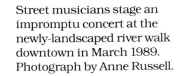

Street musicians stage an impromptu concert at the newly-landscaped river walk downtown in March 1989. Photograph by Anne Russell.

THE EIGHTIES

ball hero.

But with prosperity came growing pains. Graceful shade trees toppled as miles of asphalt widened roads and paved shopping center parking lots. Traffic throttled Market Street and College Road. Developers and preservationists manned battle stations, and the Save Masonboro Island and Save Airlie Road movements took off in earnest. Wrightsville Beach crossed the inland waterway and annexed portions of the adjacent mainland; Shell Island's giant sand dunes were leveled beneath view-obscuring condominiums; there was standing-room-only at meetings of the town council as citizens demanded stricter zoning laws. A county sign ordinance was adopted. Cape Fear country had long taken its natural assets for granted, and they were fast disappearing. The time for action was now.

By the time Wilmington's 250th birthday arrived in July 1989, the city had been featured on the "Today Show," written up in the *New York Times* and *Pace Magazine*, and recaptured its former glory as the jewel of North Carolina's coastal region.

Always the choice of oldtimers who had grown up appreciating its unique qualities, Wilmington became a haven for newcomers recently discovering that of all places to be, this was the best. The UNC-W campus expanded with impressive buildings and programs, an ice-skating arena attracted regular clientele, and fine new restaurants popped up all over town. Peripatetic Dino de Laurentiis folded his tent and slipped away, but left behind a functioning film studio and a cadre of craftsmen and technicians who like calling the Port City home. The "awesome cape" between the golden river and the mighty Atlantic greets the final decade of the twentieth century with the same vitality which has sustained it through war, pestilence, economic depression, and hurricanes. All its citizens—oldtimers, newcomers, preservationists, developers, artists, business people, government workers—do their part to keep Wilmington thriving as the most multi-faceted city in the state of North Carolina. It has come to be said that if you can't find what you're looking for in Wilmington, you're not looking very hard.

211

When the brick and granite
New Hanover County Court-
house was built in 1892 at the
corner of Princess and Third
streets on the former site of
the city animal pound, it was
called "an adornment to the
city" and became the hub of
professional and commercial
life. Its $2.2 million restora-
tion won an architectural
award in 1988. Photograph by
Anne Russell.

The New Hanover County
Commissioners hold their
first meeting in the recently-
restored courthouse, which
also houses the Wilmington
Convention and Visitors
Bureau directed by former
Bostonian Jane Peterson.
Courtesy of the *Wilmington
Star-News.*

The ceilings of the old New Hanover County Courthouse are made of stamped tin, and the arched windows are Queen Anne style. Chandeliers are replicas of the originals. The illuminated four-sided clock tower contains the original one-ton brass bell. Photograph by Joseph Ciarlanti.

213

CITY HALL   THALIAN HALL
RENOVATION AND ADDITION
VIEW FROM CHESTNUT STREET

This rendering of the Thalian Hall addition and restoration was created by Ligon Flynn Architects of Wilmington. Work is scheduled for completion in 1990. Courtesy of Thalian Hall Center for the Performing Arts.

As executive director of the Thalian Hall Center for the Performing Arts, Tony Rivenbark coordinates the restoration and addition project. Also an actor, theater director, and historian, Rivenbark has greatly expanded the budget, revenues, audiences, and number and variety of performances in the grand old hall. The Thalian Association, with Sam Garner as executive director, puts on a regular schedule of well-attended dramas and musicals. Photograph by Anne Russell.

The proscenium of Thalian Hall is undergoing restoration in the multi-million dollar architectural effort to preserve the historic theater. Courtesy of Thalian Hall Center for the Performing Arts.

214

Transplanted New Yorker Lou Criscuolo founded the Opera House Theater Company in Wilmington, which presents a regular season of musicals and drama featuring local performers at Thalian Hall and the Scottish Rite Temple. Here Criscuolo appears in *The Last of the Redhot Lovers* with Kay Joyner. Courtesy of the Opera House Theater Company.

Kay Swink, who has coordinated the restoration of St. Thomas Catholic Church on Dock Street, was the impetus behind the founding of the Playwrights Producing company in 1986. This group of Wilmington writers and actors provides readings for new scripts and mounts productions of new plays on a regular basis. Swink is the author of *Valiant Lady*, a play based on the life of Confederate spy Rose O'Neill Greenhow, to be produced during Wilmington's 250th anniversary year. Photograph by Anne Russell.

Vic Zagorski, Nancy Klase, Linda Barnes, Pete Boyle, Phil Loch, and Cynthia Dunlap performed in the romantic comedy *Good Eats*, a script developed in readings of the Playwrights Producing Company, and staged as a benefit by the Girls Club of Wilmington in February 1989. Photograph by Anne Russell.

Movie actor Tom McGovern grew up in Hackensack, New Jersey, and worked in Hollywood before coming to Wilmington in 1986 to perform in such DEG films as *Hiding Out* and *Dracula's Widow*. He founded The Actor's Workshop and was elected to the board of the Cape Fear Filmmaker's Accord, a coalition of movie-related professionals living and working in the Wilmington area. Photograph by Anne Russell.

Movie mogul Dino de Laurentiis brought DEG film studios to Wilmington and built this oceanfront house at Wrightsville Beach before departing in 1988, leaving the production facilities and the beach house as reminders of his colorful residency. Photograph by Anne Russell.

216

The Samuel H. Hughes Gallery of St. John's Museum of Art was formerly the St. Nicholas Greek Orthodox Church. The museum complex was founded in 1962 and includes historic St. John's Masonic Lodge built in 1804, and the Cowan House Studio, circa 1830, Ligon Flynn Architects has renovated and restored the structures. Courtesy of St. John's Museum of Art.

Jim Polson hosts the weekly arts program "Sounds Local" and is the cultural affairs director of Wilmington's public radio station WHQR. Friends of Public Radio organized in 1979 and went on air in April 1984 with Michael Titterton as station manager. In 1989 WHQR serves 2,000 members in a ten-county area of southeastern North Carolina with 16,000 listeners who enjoy a variety of national and local radio programs. Photograph by Anne Russell.

The University of North Carolina at Wilmington boasts a variety of highly-respected programs such as marine biology and business administration, and an expanding campus of new buildings. The University Union was built in 1983 and the William Madison Randall Library was expanded and renovated in 1987. Courtesy of the University of North Carolina at Wilmington.

Wilmington city administrator Mitzi York traveled abroad in August 1986 with an official group of local citizens on a goodwill trip to promote a sister-city relationship with Dandong, China, and to spread the word about Wilmington as an international city. Courtesy of the *Wilmington Star-News*

Dr. Gerald Shinn, popular and prolific professor in the philosophy and religion department of the University of North Carolina at Wilmington, founded the Albert Schweitzer International Prizes in 1975, which has awarded honors in medicine, music, and humanitarian endeavor to such luminaries as Mother Theresa, Andre Segovia, Beverly Sills, and Theodore Binder. The Schweitzer Prizes are a function of the North Carolina Educational, Historical, and Scientific Foundation, Inc., which has also sponsored the Museum of World Cultures at UNCW since 1981 and the publication of the pictorial history of North Carolina religions entitled *Portraits of Faith*. Photograph by Anne Russell.

219

The new Wilmington International Airport takes shape in 1988, with an adjacent 247-acre industrial park. The enlarged and improved facility will serve the rapidly-increasing flow of visitors to the Cape Fear area, and will offer support services for commercial ventures. Courtesy of the *Wilmington Star-News.*

The Railroad Museum keeps alive the days of the Atlantic Coast Line Railroad, Wilmington's transportation and economic lifeline for many decades. Local schoolteacher Hazel Morse spearheaded the effort to memorialize the train system, marshalling the resources and efforts of "Coast Line families" who create exhibits and attract visitors who share a love of railroading. The new Coast Line Convention Center is nearby. Courtesy of the *Wilmington Star-News.*

220

Susan Dillard visits Jacob's Run with her daughter Hannah, reliving memories of the popular 1980s downtown entertainment center which offered foreign films, hot bands, original drama, and tasteful dining all under one roof. The renovation to the old Manor Theater on Market Street was designed by local architect Randall Bray, with Dillard as primary investor in the project. Photograph by Anne Russell.

Front Street News proprietor Perry White provides a gathering spot for area artists and street philosophers who enjoy good reading material, conversation, music, and theatrical presentations along with a cooling beverage. Photograph by Anne Russell.

These restored houses on Second Street attest to the vigorous historic preservation effort in downtown Wilmington in the 1980s. Bed-and-breakfast inns offer charming accommodations for visitors, and grand old homes present gracious facades for passersby, as well as high-ceilinged interiors for residents. Photograph by Anne Russell.

The paddle-wheeler *Henrietta II* docks at the foot of Market Street and awaits 250th anniversary celebrants for a cruise on the Cape Fear River. The original *Henrietta* plied the river for forty years in the early 1800s. Photograph by Anne Russell.

Grace Slocum, 250th Anniversary Commission commemorative events chairman, traces her Wilmington heritage to the Holmes and Hill families of the early 1700s, and she makes her residence in the downtown historic district. Colonel Tom Price was the 250th Commission's first chairman, followed by chairman Irving Fogler. Photograph by Anne Russell.

Wilmington's Michael Jordan played basketball at Laney High School and the University of North Carolina at Chapel Hill before going with the National Basketball Association and the Chicago Bulls. The ACC Rookie of the Year won the All-American, National Player of the Year, and Eastman awards, and was a member of the U.S. Olympic Basketball Team. Photograph by Hugh Morton, courtesy of *Cape Fear Tidewater Magazine.*

Masonboro Island (right) became the focus of preservation efforts in the 1980s, as the last unspoiled oceanfront island between Wrightsville Beach and Carolina Beach. A favorite spot of boaters, picnickers, swimmers, and fishermen, Masonboro offers miles of clean white beaches, shell-collecting, swimmable sound and surf, and sheltering sand dunes. Courtesy of the *Wilmington Star-News*.

The old Crest Theater at Wrightsville Beach has been renovated into an exercise studio and a delicatessen-restaurant, while Roberts Grocery next door continues as a favorite neighborhood food shop which offers custom cuts of meat, homemade baked goods, and individual issues of the Sunday paper tagged and reserved for late-rising beach dwellers. Photograph by Anne Russell.

Pelicans on pilings ponder new condominiums on Harbor Island and inland waterway boat traffic emerging from beneath the Wrightsville Beach drawbridge. The bridge has the highest daily volume of cars on the coast and is the object of recent controversy over a suggested toll charge. Beach dwellers hope that ill-conceived idea never becomes reality and that the quality of life at Wrightsville can be preserved. Photograph by Anne Russell.

Jay DeChesere's sailboat *Papillon* is decorated with Christmas lights for the annual holiday flotilla through Banks Channel at Wrightsville Beach. Architect DeChesere's boat won first place two years in a row in the panorama, which featured fireworks, music, and, as always, attracted huge crowds to the sunset spectacle. Courtesy of Jay DeChesere.

PROFILES
IN
LEADERSHIP

Cities are in large part a reflection of the quality and success of their economic and cultural institutions and the people who manage them.

From the earliest times Wilmington has been blessed with people and institutions of foresight and tenacity. Their collective story is reflected in the preceding pages. The detailed stories of some of the best are told in the following pages.

The Publisher

GREATER WILMINGTON CHAMBER OF COMMERCE

The first Chamber of Commerce in North Carolina was organized in Wilmington in 1853, complete with a constitution and by-laws. The forty-two members paid thirty dollars in annual dues and the full-time secretary received a salary of three hundred dollars a year. Wilmington was a booming port city and the Chamber assumed the task of setting her on the right course. Chamber committees carried out objectives which related to agriculture, information and statistics, banks and currency, harbors, shipping and trading, mail and telegraph, public entertainment, conventions, civic improvements, health and sanitation, streets, and wharves.

After the outbreak of the Civil War, and North Carolina's secession from the Union, the work of the Chamber was delayed. Finally, in 1866 Wilmington again became a city by charter from the state General Assembly, and in that same year, the Chamber was officially chartered as the first in the state. During the reconstruction period, the Chamber did its part by aiding in the shipping of cotton, lumber, tobacco, and tar products. These items were shipped from the Port of Wilmington on steamers, clipper ships, and schooners to New England and Europe. In 1896, Wilmington was the largest cotton port in the country. At the close of the nineteenth century, and in the decades to follow, the Chamber of Commerce was and continues to be a driving force in the city's commercial, industrial, and residential expansion.

At the start of the twentieth century, the Chamber took an active role in promoting the area's potential for industrial development, tourism, and recreation. One way was by publishing illustrated souvenir booklets, which showcased everything from the harbor to the Carolina Yacht Club. The Chamber offered the following to prospective members of the business community:

"To those who may contemplate making Wilmington the theatre of their operations the Chamber will render every assistance and will make suitable inquiries as to possibilities for success, advantageous sites for plants, etc...."

Apparently, many took advantage of that offer. By 1903, in addition to cotton, lumber, and tar production, the city had five railway lines, two large rice mills, three daily newspapers, and a huge shipbuilding operation. As the city grew, the Chamber continued its promotion of the area. Even through the Depression, billboards, brochures, and automobile guide maps were used to encourage tourism. By the 1940s, the Chamber had renewed its efforts to entice industry into New Hanover County. A demographic profile was published, which detailed area aspects such as the labor market, cost of living, city transportation, and housing.

In the late 1950s, the Atlantic Coast Line Railroad announced its plan to relocate. This was a devastating blow

Joseph F. Augustine has served as the Executive Vice President of the Chamber since 1978.

because the railroad employed over four thousand. The business community realized decisive action was needed. In 1956, the Chamber established Wilmington's Industrial Committee of 100 and launched a formal campaign to bring new industry into the Port City. As a result, in the sixties, many major manufacturers, including General Electric, Corning, and Dupont had set up operations in Wilmington and the surrounding area.

Aside from business, the Chamber was also interested in promoting tourism and sponsored hospitality training for residents who had direct contact with the traveling public. The training focused on courtesy, giving directions, and travel suggestions. The objective of those programs was to create familiarity with the entire Cape Fear region, from the downtown riverfront to the beaches. The nation's Bicentennial celebration and an increased awareness of the environment, led the Chamber to support the restoration of the historical district and beach renourishment projects in the seventies. The Chamber's Highway Task Force also encouraged the state to complete the section of I-40 between Benson and Wilmington.

The role of the Chamber changed direction in the eighties. Attention was centered on human resources, public school programs, increasing employment opportunities for females and minorities, and enhancing the livability of the community. The Chamber continued to carry out its traditional programs, and made a concerted effort to involve a broad cross-section of business, professional, and retired citizens. Four new Chamber councils were created: Topsail Beach, Small Business, Tourism, and International Trade were added, for a total of eleven councils.

Looking to the future, the Chamber envisions two distinct areas of involvement: first, international trade emphasis through the World Trade Center, and secondly, a regional marketing strategy for all of southeastern North Carolina which includes the Marine Crescent. As Wilmington celebrates its 250th anniversary, the Chamber is totally committed to keeping this community the best place in the world to live, work, and play!

The Price-Gause House (circa 1848) has housed the Chamber since 1969. Many say the house is haunted!

ADAM & HILLIARD REALTY

CHARTER MEMBERS: Left to Right, David B. Hilliard, GRI, Broker, Owner/Partner, Helen S. Farrow, GRI, CRS, Broker, Elizabeth W. Yancey, Office Manager, and Thomas A. Adam, GRI, Principal Broker.

1989 STAFF and BROKERS: Front row left to right; Dolly Farriss, Helen Farrow, GRI, CRS, Kathy Bradford, and Margaret Sullivan. Second row; Grace Prestwood, Van Leer Rowe, Lib Yancey and Manaline Gibson. Third row; W. Murle Teachey, GRI, Dianne Stansbury and Jeff Ludwig. Fourth Row; Dave Hilliard, GRI, Leigh Hobbs, GRI, Lois Dixon, Beth Herritage, Brooks Preik and Tom Adam, GRI.

Adam and Hilliard Realty was formed October 1, 1979, by Thomas A. Adam and David B. Hilliard at 1417 South College Road in Wilmington. Tom and Dave, who previously had successful careers with other leading real estate firms, recognized a need for a company that could bring together full time, experienced real estate professionals and associate them with a locally-owned firm that specialized solely in single family residential and multi-family brokerage; thus Adam and Hilliard Realty was formed. Charter members included Thomas A. Adam, principal broker, and David B. Hilliard, partner, and two highly respected and experienced brokers, Helen S. Farrow and Betty M. Jackson. Opening its doors for the first time, Adam and Hilliard Realty, with its charter members, offered over forty-five years of real estate experience.

Originally from East Liverpool, Ohio, Tom and his wife moved to Wilmington in 1959. Tom began his successful real estate career in 1970. He served on the Board of Directors for the Wilmington Board of REALTORS from 1976 to 1985 and was treasurer of the Wilmington Board of REALTORS in 1981 and 1982. In addition, Tom was chairman of the Multiple Listing Service in 1980, and is currently a director on the Wilmington Board of REALTORS Multiple Listing Service. Tom was named "Salesman of the Year" for the Wilmington Board of REALTORS in 1977 and was "REALTOR of the Year" in 1987. Further, he is a four year veteran of the United States Army, having served in Korea. Tom graduated from Kent State University and is a graduate of the REALTORS Institute at the University of North Carolina at Chapel Hill.

A native of Wallace, North Carolina,

Dave and his wife moved to Wilmington in 1969. Dave's successful real estate career began in 1972, and he has been a strong supporter of the Wilmington Board of REALTORS, having served on their Board of Directors from 1979 to 1985. Additionally, he was vice president in 1982, president-elect in 1983, and president of the Wilmington Board of REALTORS in 1984. Dave was also honored as "Salesman of the Year" for the Wilmington Board of REALTORS in 1978 and was "REALTOR of the Year" in 1987. Dave has also served a four year term as a director for the Greater Wilmington Chamber of Commerce and is currently serving on the Board of Directors of a local bank. He is a four year veteran of the U.S. Air Force and served during the Vietnam conflict. He attended Wilmington College and graduated from the University of North Carolina at Wilmington. Dave is a graduate of the REALTORS Institute at the University of North Carolina at Chapel Hill and has served in numerous civic organizations.

In addition to the experienced staff, the company was fortunate enough to hire Elizabeth W. Yancey as its office manager. Lib had recently moved to Wilmington from Greensboro, where she had been employed by the Greater Greensboro Board of REALTORS and their Multiple Listing Service. She also had experience with a Brokerage and Appraisal firm and held a broker's license. The company immediately began to grow, adding only experienced full-time brokers to their staff. After their first year, the company was experiencing a home sale every other day. Having exceeded the company's expectations, Adam and Hilliard outgrew its original location and relocated to expanded offices at 3912 Shipyard Boulevard and con-

tinued to grow to provide real estate services to the community.

Today, Adam and Hilliard has a staff of fifteen full-time REALTOR/Brokers with over 135 years of combined experience, and still specializes in single family and multi-family home sales. The company has chosen to maintain a limited size, in order to retain its local identity and reputation, and to provide the finest professional service to the community. Believing that it should contribute to the community in the same measure that it has received, Adam and Hilliard Realty has always been a strong supporter of community activities and services. The company appreciates the unique gifts of Wilmington's past, and is committed to preserving a high quality of life in both the present and the future of our area.

Adam and Hilliard Realty is a member of the Greater Wilmington Chamber of Commerce, Wilmington Industrial and Development, Inc., "Committee of 100," and the Wilmington Cape Fear Homebuilders Association. One of the company's proudest accomplishments was being named, by its peers, Most Cooperative Multiple Listing Agency in 1980, 1982, 1983, 1985, and 1988. Adam and Hilliard Realty is a sustaining member and supporter of the Wilmington Jaycees. Tom and Dave were named "Boss of the Year" for New Hanover County in 1988 and 1989 by the Jaycees. Adam and Hilliard Realty is committed to continuing its reputation and excellence through education, dedication, professionalism and community service.

Adam and Hilliard REALTY

3912 Shipyard Blvd.
Wilmington, N.C. 28403
(919) 799-7500

ALMONT SHIPPING COMPANY

Almont Shipping Company is the direct descendent of Heide & Co., which was founded in 1870 by R. E. Heide and is one of the oldest businesses in continuous operation in New Hanover County. Sometime prior to 1925, Mr. Heide sold the company to David Scott. In 1925, David Scott sold it to W. S. R. Beane, L. B. Finberg and R. W. Cantwell. By this time, Heide & Co. was composed of two very distinct strong operating departments—general cargo which made use of North Carolina State Ports facilities, and bulk cargo which was handled through the company's privately owned facilities.

In 1965 the company spun off the general cargo division, which along with the name Heide & Co., was sold to Luckenbach Steamship Co. (presently operating as Lavino Shipping Company), and renamed the remaining bulk handling facility Almont Shipping Com-

pany. Mr. Beane had previously bought out his partners and in 1983 the latest change in ownership took place when Almont employees purchased the company from Mr. Beane.

Almont specializes in stevedoring, storing and distributing imported dry bulk commodities. Bulk commodities are those which do not require crating or packing, and can be discharged from vessels using bucket, conveyor or pneumatic methods. Almont takes advantage of each method, but most often discharges cargo from ships using a bridge-type bucket unloader. Cargo is lifted from the vessel into hoppers which feed several miles of conveyor systems to storage, both outside and into warehouses.

Located on the Northeast/Cape Fear River at mile 28, with a navigable depth of 35 feet of fresh water, the Almont facility makes use of approximately 43

acres of waterfront property. Of the seven warehouses presently in use, three were built in 1904, two were added during the 1960s, another was added in 1978, and another in 1980. The company offices were located at Brunswick Street until 1959 when they were moved to Highway 421 North.

After 28 years on the West Bank of the Northeast/Cape Fear River, the offices were once again moved to the city into an old remodeled Coastline Freight Station building at One Hanover Street.

Currently under the leadership of Estell C. Lee as president, Almont Shipping Company looks forward to provide the best customer service available anywhere in the world, to be an exceptionally good community citizen, and to continue strong, positive growth. This outlook and the 50 dedicated employees are the backbone of a strong client-oriented business.

ANDREW & KUSKE CONSULTING ENGINEERS

John R. Andrew Consulting Engineer was founded on May 9, 1983, by John R. "Rod" Andrew. Several months later J.A. "Jack" Kuske became a partner in the firm and Andrew & Kuske Consulting Engineers, Inc., was formed. With over forty-five years of combined experience in the construction and engineering practice, Andrew and Kuske had a strong desire to own and operate their own business utilizing their broad previous experience.

Mr. Andrew is a graduate of North Carolina State University with a master of science degree and is a registered professional engineer in North Carolina, Virginia, South Carolina, Georgia and Florida. Mr. Kuske is a graduate of the University of Illinois with a bachelor of science degree in civil engineering with structural option. He is a registered professional engineer in North Carolina, Virginia, South Carolina, Georgia, Florida and Illinois. He is also a registered structural engineer in Illinois.

The firm has excelled in a variety of projects including the design of buildings of reinforced concrete, structural steel, masonry and timber; computer methods and systems for the solution of structural problems and cost control; design of highways, bridges, and historical structures; and design and analysis of wharves, piers and docking facilities. The firm has also become accomplished in the design of utility systems for municipalities, including: water, sanitary sewer and storm drainage, design of ground storage tanks, pile foundations, earth fill structures, industrial utility waste treatment and collection control facilities.

Mr. Andrew and Mr. Kuske are members of the National Society of Professional Engineers and the American Society of Civil Engineers. Mr. Andrew is a member of the Professional Engineers of North Carolina, Consulting Engineers Council, and the American Concrete Institute. He is presently vice-chairman of the Building Code Council for the state of North Carolina, a member of the American Arbitration Association, and a member of the National Academy of Forensic Engineers. He also served as president of the Chamber of Commerce.

Mr. Kuske is a member of the North Carolina Society of Engineers and the Professional Engineers of North Carolina and Consulting Engineers Council. He also served on the board of directors for both the Brigade Boys' Club and the Wilmington Rotary Club and was a charter member on the board of directors for the Sertoma Club.

Andrew & Kuske Consulting Engineers, Inc. looks forward to the future and continues to provide the finest in professional engineering services to their clients, both promptly and at reasonable fees.

BELK BEERY COMPANY, INC.

JAMES C. WILLIAMS

W. B. BEERY, JR.

Belk Beery, the Wilmington department store, opened its doors in 1915 as Belk Williams Company. James C. Williams made the arrangements to open a new Wilmington store for the Belk Brothers Co. located in Charlotte. Williams, a native of Union County, went to work for William Henry Belk and Dr. John M. Belk in Charlotte; he became manager of the Wilmington store when it opened in October 1915. Under Williams' leadership the Belk Williams Company expanded until it occupied three adjoining buildings on Front Street.

W. B. Beery, Jr. joined Belk Williams in 1919, and worked his way to assistant store manager. He became manager of the store after Williams' death in 1943. Belk Williams continued to increase in size and products offered. In 1951 the first truly modern department store, complete with escalators, spot lighting and spacious displays, opened at Second and Chestnut streets, under a new name—Belk Beery.

W. B. Beery III joined his father in 1946, and the successful father and son management team lasted until 1961. W. B. Beery III founded and assumed leadership of Belk Beery Services in 1970. Today, Belk Beery, located at Independence Mall has completely evolved from a country store to that of a fashion trend-setter.

While Belk Beery continues to provide Wilmington with the newest in fashion and other products, it also provides Wilmington with a sense of its heritage. Wilmington's history, culture and environs are the theme of the nine giant mosaic murals welcoming shoppers to the Belk Beery store. The colorful arch-shaped mosaics were translated from original watercolors painted by Wilmington artist Samuel D. Bissette. Measuring 15 by 17 feet each, they are among the largest groups of mosaics in the United States. By day or night the Belk Beery entrances stand as a prominent salute to the port city. As it continues to offer the best in fashion and quality service, Belk Beery is always proud of the people in Wilmington that it serves.

BLAND & ASSOCIATES REALTORS

Elizabeth W. Bland, GRI-CRS-CRB, owner of Bland & Associates, REALTORS,® was recognized as "Entrepreneur of the Year" in 1987. Having established her firm in 1979 and building three office buildings by September 1988, she embodies her belief in property ownership for financial growth. The buildings at 4106-4110 Shipyard Boulevard, Wilmington, North Carolina, house her offices as well as other professional tenants. The building at 107 W. Salisbury Street, Wrightsville Beach, North Carolina, serves as their beach and resort office. Future plans include a fourth building for lease purposes at this site.

Bland & Associates, REALTORS,® is a full service real estate firm serving New Hanover, Pender, and Brunswick counties with twenty-seven licensed associates who are full-time professionals. As a designated "Homequity Relocation Center," Bland & Associates, REALTORS,® through their Homequity Relocation Service affiliation offers expert assistance for those moving to other areas of the country. Homequity has over 3,500 broker member offices from coast to coast. Relocation assistance is a top priority for Bland & Associates, as is working closely with local industry and community organizations.

Over twenty years of experience in the Wilmington area has given Bland & Associates the capability to handle the needs of local buyers, retirees, transferees, and second home buyers with professional expertise and individual attention.

Bland & Associates, REALTORS,® is a proud example of what dedication and professionalism can accomplish in our free enterprise system as they continue to seek new ways to serve the Wilmington/Wrightsville Beach area in its continued growth.

CAPE INDUSTRIES

Cape Industries is a quality supplier of industrial chemicals with which other well-known firms manufacture a broad array of polyester products. A joint venture company of majority owner Hoechst Celanese Corporation and American Petrofina, Cape Industries' major customers are 3M Co., Firestone, Allied-Signal, BASF, Imperial Chemical Industries PLC and majority parent Hoechst Celanese.

First begun in 1967 as Hercules, Inc. and housing 80 employees, Hercules merged with American Petrofina in September of 1976 and the company became Hercofina. On May 29, 1985, Hercules sold their interest to Hoechst Celanese and the company name was changed to Cape Industries. Today, Cape Industries has 391 employees and 179 contract maintenance, security and janitorial personnel.

Located on a portion of a 1,600 acre site along U.S. 421 near Wilmington, Cape Industries produces dimethyl terephthalate and terephthalic acid. These chemicals are used in the making of polyester fibers for textile, apparel and home furnishings applications; tire cord, carpeting, geotextiles, polyester film for x-ray and photographic films and video and audio tapes; and polyester resins for beverage bottles and engineering resins. Also produced at Cape Industries is Terate (R) resins which are used in the manufacture of foam insulation. Raw materials for the Cape Industries operation are floated up the adjacent Cape Fear River on barges. Export shipments are processed through the state ports to destinations all over the world.

Cape Industries president, R.L. Guard, attributes the company's achievement and maintenance of its worldwide outreach to the constant pursuit of four fundamental Hoechst Celanese and Petrofina objectives. "These objectives," he says, "involve making quality products as safely and as cost efficiently as possible, while involving employees to the fullest possible extent.

"Just as strong as our commitment to maintaining a safe, pleasant working environment for Cape Industries employees is the Hoechst Celanese and Petrofina commitment to environmental, health and safety protection for our customers, neighbors and others who may be affected by our products or activities. In short, being a good neighbor, as well as a good employer and a quality supplier of industrial chemicals, is a responsibility we take quite seriously."

Cape Industries is an equal opportunity employer and is committed to the effective and full utilization of all its employees.

CAPE FEAR MEMORIAL HOSPITAL

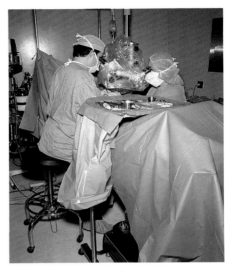

Outpatient services in radiology and respiratory therapy have been greatly expanded. With its Back School and Industrial Rehabilitation program, the hospital's Physical Therapy Department is a leader in occupational health services to business and industry. The hospital's Lifeline project serves senior citizens in their homes and, for eight years, Lower Cape Fear Hospice, a program serving terminally ill patients and their families, was housed on hospital grounds.

While plans are being prepared to enlarge the hospital to meet any future community demands upon its services, Cape Fear Memorial Hospital stands today as a full-service, modern medical-surgical institution, fully accredited in service to all people. Says the executive director, Joseph L. Soto: "Cape Fear Memorial Hospital has grown from a small, traditional facility into a thriving community hospital. Our growth has translated into major accomplishments in health care services—same day and ambulatory surgery, special medical testing, chronic pain control, Women's Services, health promotion, a new Emergency Center, a new Intensive Care Unit, and Family Birthing Center. As the hospital continues to expand and incorporate the latest biomedical technology, we are guided by our founders' original commitment to excellent medical care, human compassion, and personalized service."

Patients at Cape Fear Memorial have traditionally been treated "like family" and the hospital is not only well known for its warm friendly atmosphere, but for its excellent tradition of medical care.

In 1956, three Wilmington doctors, W. C. Mebane, R. T. Sinclair, Jr. and S. E. Pace, envisioning an institution providing medical and surgical service to the community, purchased the Wessell Sanitorium on Wrightsville Avenue from New Hanover County. Chartered June 7, 1956, as a non-profit, non-denominational hospital to be operated by a Board of Trustees, and opened to the public in 1957, the old sanitorium was completely renovated, with the installation of forty-three beds, an operating theatre, an x-ray department, a clinical laboratory, and other necessary equipment to create a full-service hospital.

By 1958, Cape Fear Memorial Hospital was accredited by the Joint Commission of American Hospitals, a distinction it continues to hold today. Since then, Cape Fear Memorial Hospital has grown from a small hospital employing fifty-five people into a sprawling 142-bed medical center that employs nearly 500 persons, and has 160 physicians on staff.

The hospital's earliest origins can be traced to when Dr. Ernest S. Bullock constructed a small private hospital on Front Street. As demand for hospital services grew, there was some sentiment for expanding the public James Walker Memorial Hospital and incorporating the 26-bed Bullock Hospital Clinic. But Dr. Sinclair and his partners decided to dissolve the clinic and start the private, non-profit facility instead. On the evening of August 6, 1957, two dozen patients were moved from Bullock Hospital downtown to the new facility outside the city, named Cape Fear Memorial Hospital. An appendectomy was performed early the next morning in the new operating room.

Cape Fear Memorial Hospital has responded to the health care needs of a growing community with many innovative programs and services. The high cost of staying in the hospital spurred a new ambulatory surgery program.

CAROLINA POWER & LIGHT COMPANY

CP&L's Eastwood office opened in October 1987 at 1700 Eastwood Road. The Eastwood office serves 24,000 customers in the eastern portions of New Hanover, Pender and Onslow counties. The downtown Wilmington office serves 47,000 customers.

Wilmington received electricity for street lighting on March 1, 1886. The power was generated by a small plant operated at the machine shop of Burr & Bailey, located in the block surrounded by Front, Second, Market, and Dock streets. A few months later the city's power supplier was incorporated under the name of the Wilmington Electric Lighting Company. After two more sales, Wilmington's seacoast railroad, gas company and street railways merged to form Consolidated Railways, Light & Power Company. The man behind the merger was Hugh MacRae, president of the Wilmington Gas Light Company. MacRae's aim was to consolidate the railways, light and power facilities into one operation.

MacRae organized the Tide Water Power Company in Wilmington, in February 1907 to finance the tremendous expansion of his utilities. Tide Water purchased the properties of Consolidated Railways and Light & Power Company and became the only public service corporation in the South whose common stock was entirely held in its hometown. MacRae owned fifty-three percent of the common stock.

In the 1920s Tide Water Power Company grew rapidly and made interconnections with Carolina Power & Light Company for system reliability. In 1952 Tide Water merged with CP&L. Tide Water's small generating plants were shut down when CP&L completed the L. V. Sutton coal-fired generating plant near Wilmington in 1954.

Today, Carolina Power & Light Company is an investor-owned electric utility company, which serves an area of approximately 30,000 square miles. The area includes a substantial portion of the coastal plains in North Carolina extending to the Atlantic coast between the Pamilco River and the South Carolina border, the lower Piedmont section in North Carolina, the Pee Dee area of South Carolina, and an area in western North Carolina in and around the city of Asheville.

CP&L's Eastwood office is uniquely different from the company's other offices in the Carolinas. The office was designed to capture a bit of history and heritage of the area and the Lumina pavilion was an influence in its architecture. Lumina was an entertainment palace built by Tide Water Power Company in the early 1900s to attract more visitors to Wrightsville Beach. The Eastwood office's colors and building materials were chosen to blend in with the area and the growth that is expected.

CP&L has responded to customer concern about rising prices by introducing energy-saving programs. Today the company is a leader in the promotion of energy conservation and load management. Building on the strength of the past, CP&L is working to assure reliable supplies of electricity to power the continuing progress of the Carolinas.

COAST LINE CENTER

Preserving a most significant era in Wilmington's history, the Coast Line Center sits at the site of the rail head and home offices of the old Atlantic Coast Line Railroad, the longest rail line of its day. Ideally located to attract tourists and business travelers alike, the Coast Line Center is only minutes from inviting coastal beaches, and within walking distance to the central business district in the heart of historic downtown Wilmington, a picturesque community of cultural and historic attractions, fine dining, shopping, and entertainment.

Designed to meet the fast growing needs of the traveler and tourist, as well as the local and regional markets, the Coast Line Center consists of a 12,000 square foot convention center for trade shows, conventions, exhibits, and meetings. Also featured is the newly constructed Coast Line Inn, which encompasses fifty-one beautiful rooms and suites, all with river views. An executive conference room, and a multi-level tower suite complete the inn. Ferrovia, an exquisitely designed restaurant, offers fine dining, a complete bar, banquet and catering facilities, and live entertainment. On a larger scale, Coast Line Center engages live entertainment featuring everything from the Glen Miller Orchestra to Beatlemania. Other attractions include the Coast Line Cafe, a casual deli pub in a railroad atmosphere, and unique and charming "platform" shops. All have a spectacular view of the scenic Cape Fear River.

The riverfront provides the backdrop for regular outdoor art and music festivals. The colorful Azalea Festival in the spring and Riverfest in the fall attract thousands of attendants yearly. Other tourist attractions of note are the Railroad Museum featuring antique locomotive, caboose, and train memorabilia while one of the state's foremost tourist draws—World War II's impressive battleship, the U.S.S. *North Carolina*—is located directly across the river and annually attracts over 250,000 visitors. The Coast Line Center's courtyard and deck on the Riverwalk offer another staging arena for celebrations and promotional events. The scenic Riverwalk will eventually connect the Coast Line Center with Riverfront Park in historic downtown Wilmington.

Coast Line Associates, founders of the Coast Line Center, have contributed greatly to the growth potential in the Wilmington area. This strong project

team consists of Faison Kuester, Jr., and William T. Baird of Kuester Development Corporation in Charlotte; DeWayne Anderson and Bill Benton of Anderson, Benton and Company in Winston-Salem; and David Weil of Weil Enterprises in Goldsboro. With years of experience in a diversity of real estate developments, they have individually and collectively invested in major rehabilitation projects throughout the downtown area, including the ten-story First Union Bank building, the Cape Fear Hotel, and the $7.5 million Coast Line Center.

The Coast Line Center recalls the importance the Atlantic Coast Line

Railroad has played in Wilmington's economic development. Those innovative, new uses of the historic old railroad reclaim "Coast Line" as a thriving center of daily commerce and create a delightful setting for combining business and pleasure.

CORNING INCORPORATED

Corning Incorporated opened their plant in Wilmington, North Carolina in 1966, beginning another division in their continuing success story of the business established by Amory Houghton and others in 1851. Corning Glass Works established themselves in Corning, New York in 1868. It is now a corporation with thirty-four plants worldwide (twenty-four in the United States), 60,000 manufactured products, 27,000 employees and sales in excess of 2.1 billion. Corning is composed of four major business sectors: Specialty Glass and Ceramics, Consumer Housewares, Laboratory Sciences, and Telecommunications.

After several years of geographic research, the decision was made that a Corning production facility would be located in the Wilmington area. The plant was initially devoted to the pro-

duction of electrical resistors for use in electronic circuits that were used in television sets and computers. A work force of two hundred and fifty was initially employed in the production of the high performance electronic components.

In 1978, plans to phase out the resistor operations and begin the production of optical fibers at the Wilmington plant, as part of the Telecommunications Products Division, were implemented. Corning's facility in Wilmington is now among the world's largest optical fiber manufacturing facilities. A ninety-seven million dollar expansion was made to help meet the continued demand for the product. A work force of approximately eight hundred is employed to effectively operate this facility. The plant now has the capacity to produce 720,000 miles of the pure glass thread.

As one of the largest employers in the New Hanover County area, Corning/Wilmington adheres to the policy of community involvement by supporting various local civic and charitable groups, as well as education and the arts.

Corning and all of the Wilmington employees are proud of their leadership in the development of the optical fiber product. Our goal is to continue developing to meet the continued growth of the telecommunications and data communications market requirements.

All Corning employees from the plant floor to the executive office, take part in our Total Quality system that embraces both products and the individual performance. Always in step with the times, Corning will continue to lead in telecommunications technology.

EASTERN DELIVERY SERVICE, INC.

Eastern Delivery Service was founded on June 1, 1977 by Katherine Scott Bell Moore and her former husband, Milton. In 1978, the business was incorporated and Mrs. Moore became the sole stockholder. The home office is located on Castle Hayne Road and a second office is located in Kinston.

Eastern specializes in "exclusive use" hauling, which involves delivering in crises, machine parts and other equipment for the daily maintenance and upkeep of an industry. ("Exclusive" means that a shipper in a hurry pays for the use of an entire truck even though his cargo doesn't fill it.) The company also does contract mail service, bus and air freight deliveries, wholesaler distribution and retail store deliveries. The company is licensed by the N.C. Utilities Commission for statewide operations and by the Interstate Commerce Commission for East Coast operations. Eastern also handles time sensitive and emergency shipments that prevent plant shut downs when equipment is needed and provides voluntary transportation for the local food bank.

Mrs. Moore has a bachelor's degree from the University of North Carolina at Wilmington in English, speech and drama, and started her career as a teacher. She taught in the public schools in New Hanover and Pender counties; at Central Piedmont Community College and Charlotte; and at Cape Fear Technical Institute. Mrs. Moore comes from a prominent black Wilmington family. Her uncle, Armond W. Scott, was the first black federally appointed judge, named by President Franklin D. Roosevelt.

Mrs. Moore has continued her family's long service to her city. She is cochairman of Citizens for a Better Wilmington, former chairman of the New Hanover Human Relations Commission. She is a member of the board of directors of Committee of 100, Carolina Savings Bank, Duke University LEAD program, and the Department of Social Services. She has served on the Governor's Advisory Council on Women in Economic Development, the Lieutenant Governor's Commission on Jobs and the Economy, and the boards of North Carolina Equity, the United Way, Salvation Army, and the Thalians. Mrs. Moore received the 1985 YWCA Women of Achievement award in business, the 1985 Links Achievement award, and was second runner up for the 1985 U.S. Small

Business Administration Minority Business Person award.

Looking forward to the future, Eastern Delivery Service and Katherine B. Moore look forward to providing reliable emergency and contract delivery service at a sensible price.

E.I. DuPONT De NEMOURS & COMPANY

The Cape Fear site of the Du Pont Company, located in Brunswick County, began operation in July 1968, producing Dacron® polyester staple. In July 1970, Dacron® polyester yarn production started and in June 1973, production started for dimethyl terephthalate (DMT), the primary ingredient of polyester fiber.

Du Pont currently has approximately 1,500 employees, including over 1,100 production employees and about 400 technical, supervisory and clerical employees. The annual payroll in 1988 was $60 million. The plant covers 2,215 acres and pays more than $1 million each year in Brunswick County property taxes. This represents approximately 10% of all the property tax paid in the county.

Du Pont purchased 100% of the plant's electricity from Carolina Power & Light Company, the annual usage being about the same as a city of 35,000 to 40,000 persons. Along with the electricity purchased from CP&L, the plant's power house supplies a significant portion of the energy needs. It is capable of supplying steam heat for a city of about 50,000. A significant portion of the new power house investment provides environmental control facilities necessary for burning coal. The water supply is from the Cape Fear River and wells. The daily pumping rate is equivalent to

about half that of Wilmington's water requirements. Facilities for treating water taken from the Cape Fear River would be capable of serving a city of about 85,000 people.

The Du Pont plant waste water treatment facilities would handle waste of a city the size of Charlotte. It is considered by the EPA and the State of North Carolina as one of the best in the state. No. 6 fuel oil is supplied by Exxon through a 14.2 mile pipeline. Annual usage would provide heat for every home in the city of Wilmington. Process and comfort is all electrical and is about the same amount as 7,500 average size homes.

Du Pont's safety and health policy assures that its products can be made, distributed and used in a manner that protects the environment and the health and safety of its employees, customers and the public. According to OSHA statistics, the employees of the Cape Fear site are 17 times safer than the national average for the chemical industry and 68 times safer than industry as a whole. In short, employees are safer at work than at home.

One full-time physician and one physician assistant are employed at the Cape Fear site along with five nurses, to help ensure a healthy workplace. Each employee receives a complete physical examination at least every three years

and employees over 50 years old are examined yearly. A Hearing Conservation Program of annual hearing tests is in place for all individuals exposed to 85 dba and above. Two technical employees are assigned as Occupational Health Specialists to monitor the workplace.

The coal-fired boilers completed in late 1982 use the latest technology for industrial boilers to control emissions and minimize any negative impact on the environment. Fibers operations use 36% less energy (electric, fuel oil, steam, etc.) today per pound of product than in 1972. This reduction has been accomplished through employee involvement and dedication in changing operating instructions, product conversion, and recovering heat versus venting to the atmosphere.

Petrochemical facilities use less energy to produce a pound of product today than in 1972. Continuing efforts to reduce energy consumption will result in consuming less than half of the energy to make a pound of product than was needed ten years ago. This energy savings of the Petrochemicals operation is enough to supply 50,000 average American homes for a year. These savings were made possible by energy-conscious equipment design and operating techniques, and the deliberate dedicated effort of all employees.

FEDERAL PAPER BOARD COMPANY

At sunset, the Riegelwood mill.

A 24-ton reel of paper, just manufactured on No. 15 Paper Machine, one of two paper machines at Riegelwood Operations.

Federal Paper Board Company was founded by William Shortess in 1916, with one plant in Bogata, New Jersey. From these humble beginnings Federal has grown to become one of the largest producers of bleached, coated paperboard and bleached market pulp in the United States, and now ranks in the top five U.S. corporations producing quality lumber products. The market pulp and paperboard mill at Riegelwood, North Carolina, is a major profit center in the corporation. Federal also operates twenty-one other manufacturing facilities which are scattered nationwide, and in the United Kingdom, and maintains offices in London, Tokyo, and Zurich.

John R. Kennedy, Sr., along with two associates acquired the company following the death of Mr. Shortess in 1942. Folding carton and recycled paperboard plants were added, and in 1954, Federal went public on the New York Stock Exchange. It was in January 1972 that the company acquired the Riegelwood mill and the Woodlands Division in southeastern North Carolina. This marked Federal's entry into the southeastern U.S. forest products industry. Federal has since purchased another bleached paperboard mill in Augusta, Georgia, dramatically increasing the bleached paperboard production capacity.

One would be hard pressed, nowadays, to go through the day without encountering *something* made of paperboard. In the supermarket we find dozens of products packaged in paperboard. From pasta to pantyhose, cigarette cartons to computer disk covers; all are packaged using Federal products. Bookstores and card shops dis-play items made from Federal's printing grades.

"We are a customer-oriented company dedicated to serving the needs of our customers," says Vice-President of the Riegelwood Operations, Dr. Kirk Semke. "Quality is foremost. Our reputation will continue to be built on the quality of our products."

Says Dr. Semke, "At Federal, our commitment is to the development of those resources which are and will be the building blocks of our future success. This commitment is built on the quest for excellence in the manufacture of both bleached paperboard and market pulp This has brought us to the position which we enjoy today, that of one of the largest producers of bleached paperboard and market pulp in the United States."

At the Riegelwood mill, Federal manufactures bleached, coated paperboard on two modern machines, as well as high quality market pulp on the very large "Carolina King" pulp dryer. Paperboard is produced at the rate of 900 tons per day and is marketed for printing and packaging end-uses of a variety of domestic products. More than 50 percent of the approximately 1,350 tons per day of market pulp is exported for use in overseas markets. Federal also operates a modern lumber manufacturing facility at nearby Armour, North Carolina, which produces quality untreated lumber for the growing southeastern United States lumber market.

Locally, Federal contributes nearly $200 million in wages, salaries, and services to the economy, earning Federal employees some of the best wages in southeastern North Carolina

In conjunction with Local 738 of the United Paperworkers International Union, Federal jointly sponsors the Federal Employees Community Fund each year. Over the past twenty-eight years, the fund has contributed hundreds of thousands of dollars to charities and non-profit service organizations in southeastern North Carolina and across the United States. this program is conducted in the fall of the year (similar to the United Way Campaign). In the 1988 campaign, employees donated over $125,000 to this fund.

The work environment at Federal stresses freedom, participation, and open communication, and has helped Federal remain prosperous and innovative. "We recognize the value of honest, enterprising individuals," says Semke. "Federal has grown as a direct result of the contributions and initiatives of our employees over the years. By further developing opportunities for our employees, we will sustain the momentum created by their dedication and hard work."

One of the innovative quality programs begun at Riegelwood is the Statistical Quality Improvement Program. This highly successful program was pioneered for the pulp and paper industry at the Riegelwood mill and has set industry-wide standards.

Growth is definitely part of the future plans for Federal. In 1989, the company purchased a paper mill in Inverurie, Scotland. The company is expanding its Augusta Operations, which will increase its ability to penetrate the bleached board market in the United States.

FISHER & COMPANY

CERTIFIED PUBLIC ACCOUNTANTS

When you enter the offices of Fisher & Company, CPA's, you're sure to notice a difference. The office is comfortable and you are welcomed warmly. The professionals and staff seem to have the notion that they are there because you are. You begin to feel that this is the place you can bring your problems and find someone anxious to help you solve them. In a word, you feel you are about to receive SERVICE.

Fisher & Company was founded in

Fisher & Company offices at 5030 New Centre Drive in Wilmington.

Tony and Roger Fisher, Original partners of Fisher & Company, CPA's.

1979 in Wilmington, when Tony Fisher established a sole proprietorship in a small office complex on College Road near the University of North Carolina at Wilmington. Drawing on experience gained from past associations with other CPA's, and having learned what to do as well as what not to do, he began to formulate a master plan on how a CPA firm should be managed. Tony's different approach to accounting was evident from the start. With the notion that personal service should be given in one's relationship with his CPA, he developed a firm philosophy emphasizing high standards, quality work, fair billings and the clients best interest at the heart of each engagement. A second ingredient was Tony's commitment to technology. He envisioned that the efficiencies necessary to best serve his clients would come only from computerization and he was determined to stay at the leading edge on this front.

In order to accomplish his objectives, Tony recognized that he must surround himself with competent professionals, who, in exchange for a good place to work, recognition as individuals and treatment as professionals, would help the firm thrive and prosper.

In 1984, Tony invited his brother Roger to join him in the practice, and on January 1, 1986 they formed a partnership. Similar philosophies of client service and a lifelong chemistry between the brothers became the natural ingredients for success. Together they refined the firm philosophy and directed the firm's growth in the management services area for closely held businesses. Recognition of the worth of the individual, whether client or staff member, continues as the cornerstone of that philosophy.

Fisher & Company, CPA's looks forward to the future of Wilmington with enthusiasm and anticipation. Tony and Roger appreciate their good fortune in having found Wilmington as the place they would settle and begin their business. As Wilmington emerges into the 21st century, so will Fisher & Company, with its different approach toward finding better financial solutions. A different attitude, and a different approach will keep Fisher & Company among the leaders of its industry in Wilmington and North Carolina.

GE-WILMINGTON NUCLEAR FUEL AND AIRCRAFT ENGINES

There are people in North Carolina—even a few in Wilmington—who think GE makes lightbulbs at its facility on Hwy. 117, about 2 miles north of the city. In some ways, that's understandable. As one of the world's largest and most rapidly evolving companies, it's often hard to keep up with all of the things GE does provide for America and the world. And within New Hanover County are state-of-the-art facilities producing aircraft engine parts and fuel for nuclear power plants.

GE chose the site, a largely forested tract of more than 1,600 acres, 21 years ago. It became the manufacturing arm of GE's nuclear energy business based in San Jose, California. In 1968 the plant shipped its first nuclear fuel bundles—uranium fuel pellets packed in rods that are bundled in a configuration designed to accommodate the coolant, water. The Nuclear Fuel and Components Manufacturing (NF&CM) facility remains a model of power technology today. In February of 1989, for example, yet another improved bundle design made its debut—and more are in development.

But as the market for nuclear fuel narrowed, it became evident that GE would have to find new ways to protect the jobs of NF&CM employees.

At the same time, GE's thriving Aircraft Engines (AE) business sought to expand its operations based in Evendale, Ohio. The existence of easily converted plant space and a highly skilled workforce, especially in the machine trades, made Wilmington attractive. In 1980, Wilmington's Rotating Parts division was created to produce rotating parts for commercial and military aircraft engines. As the need for more employees grew, employees from NF&CM adapted their skills to the needs of Aircraft Engines. The two sides of the house grew together.

Today that is all the more evident. Plant services such as benefits administration, the on-site medical unit, the cafeteria, the plant newspaper, and company outings reflect a site-wide orientation. As the marketplace of today is increasingly a global one, GE employees understand the need to work together, even if they are involved in two largely unrelated businesses. The plant employs just over 2,300 people, about equally divided between the two businesses.

Each business is facing unique challenges. GE's Aircraft Engines group now serves more and more commercial airlines, having been heavily oriented toward defense contracting initially. The wisdom of this repositioning is this year becoming most apparent: While defense growth is expected to flatten, GE in February landed its largest contract ever—a 200 engine deal with American Airlines expected to run well into the 1990s.

Wilmington's NF&CM operation, while anticipating level employment, works to outmaneuver new worldwide competitors. Conglomerates created through the mergers of European firms and such powerhouses as Exxon challenge GE's hold on nuclear fuel leadership. The primary marketplaces are not just the United States; Europe relies on nuclear power as do the Japanese. (GE-Wilmington NF&CM representatives, including hourly employees, make frequent trips to Japan.)

Employee involvement and innovations are taking both AE and NF&CM into the 1990s. Highly motivated "Self-Directed Teams" lead the charge in highly competitive nuclear fuel markets. Self-directed workteams set the pace for Aircraft Engines.

Said one employee, "We feel like we're the best, and we intend to do what it takes to stay that way."

HARBOUR ASSOCIATES

Harbour Associates, one of the largest commercial and residential development companies in North Carolina, was founded in 1969 by Joseph R. Reaves and Malcolm T. Murray. An ambitious project of the partners was the development of The Cotton Exchange, an eight-building complex of shops, restaurants and offices located on Wilmington's historic waterfront.

Occupying two city blocks, the property had been slated for demolition during urban renewal efforts. While much of Wilmington's downtown district was being abandoned, Reaves and Murray recognized the potential of the area. The architectural and historical significance of the buildings provided the impetus for Harbour Associates to examine several possible uses for the property. After extensive research into the idea of making the buildings into a theme shopping center, Reaves and Murray moved ahead with five years of intensive efforts to make the possibility into a reality.

Just before Reaves and Murray took title to the property, a tremendous fire gutted the center section. On June 20, 1974, the partners watched as walls collapsed and the project's potential appeared to diminish. In August of 1975, however, they decided to proceed. The fire had actually provided the men with new ideas in terms of creating a Front Street entrance and a landscaped courtyard. In the midst of bulldozers clearing debris, burned out timbers and fallen walls, Reaves and Murray shared their vision with prospective merchants. Courtley's Deli opened on the Nutt Street level of the Granary Building just in time for the Azalea Festival in 1976. It was followed by The Granary, The Sampler and The Ship's Store. With two levels of one building occupied, The Cotton Exchange became an instant attraction for curious Wilmingtonians.

Restoration was done with an emphasis on maintaining the historical integrity of the buildings. The name of the project itself was chosen because the buildings housed the Alexander Sprunt & Son Company in the middle 1800s. At that time, Sprunt was the largest exporter of cotton in the world. The Cotton Exchange was, for Reaves and Murray, an appropriate name and theme for the complex.

Today, The Cotton Exchange is a thriving shopping, dining and office center with twenty-eight specialty shops and restaurants. It is the single largest unit of redeveloped retail property in downtown Wilmington, attracting business to and benefiting from an increasingly robust and revitalized commercial and residential neighborhood. Reaves and Murray continue to plan development for The Cotton Exchange and oversee its daily operation.

Approaching retirement, the partners placed Harbour Associates in the hands of Stephen H. Davenport, Jr., who relocated to Wilmington from Charlotte, North Carolina, and brought Harbour Associates under the umbrella of Davenport Properties on June 2, 1986. Reaves and Murray are on the Board of Directors of Harbour Development and Management and the commercial division of Harbour occupies the third floor of the Alexander Sprunt Building on North Front Street in The Cotton Exchange.

The Cotton Exchange offers unusual merchandise at competitive prices. Old-fashioned values combined with friendly service make shopping and visiting a leisurely pleasure. Harbour Associates and The Cotton Exchange look forward to a vital progressive future in Wilmington.

HIERONYMUS SEAFOOD RESTAURANT

Founded by L.G. (Glenn) Hieronymus in New Hanover County with just twelve employees on August 1, 1972, Hieronymus Seafood Restaurant grew out of earlier successful efforts at commercial fishing and retail and wholesale seafood distribution, and now employs sixty-five. With an eye toward quality and service, all seafood is locally harvested, served fresh, and gives residents and tourists alike the opportunity to taste the wide varieties of foods available from the Atlantic Ocean, while showcasing the difference that "fresh" makes.

In the spirit of public service, Glenn Hieronymus has played a key role in civic and state affairs. He is a member of the South Atlantic Management Council, North Carolina Marina Cresent, the 200 Mile Board, the American Cancer Association, the North Carolina Arthritis Foundation, Hospice, the Boy Scouts of America, and the American Heart Association.

Hieronymus Seafood Restaurant also offers organically grown produce, fresh spices, homemade breads, desserts, sauces, and side dishes. Future plans for development will be in the area of quality and service, long a staple of the Hieronymus name. With the slogan of "Seafood fresh from our boats," Hieronymus's goal will continue to be bringing good food from our oldest industry—the harvesting of the sea.

LANDFALL

landfall's page in history

Once the centerpiece for one of the Jones estate's formal gardens, the temple garden remains as a reminder of the days of grandeur.

Landfall may be new as a residential community, but people have been talking about it for over four hundred years. In fact, the property has a history as rich and varied as its landscape.

On February 20, 1524, Giovanni da Verrazzano and his crew of fifty sailed into sight of the North Carolina coast after a tempestuous voyage across the Atlantic from Portugal. Verrazzano's compass readings and his account of the historic arrival lead us to believe that the shores he first saw are what we call Landfall today.

"And sailing forwards, we found certain small rivers and arms of the sea, that fall down by certain creeks, washing the shore on both sides as the coast lieth. And beyond this we saw the open country rising in height above the sandy shores with many fair fields and plains, full of mighty great woods, some very thick, and some thin, replenished with diverse sorts of trees, as pleasant and delectable to behold, as is possible to imagine."

The land became the subject of more discussion around the turn of the twentieth century, this time of a more social than geographic nature. In 1902, the property was acquired by wealthy rice and railway baron, Pembroke Jones, for a game reserve. It was christened Pembroke Park.

Pembroke Jones, history tells us, was not a man to do things in a small way. Jones and his wife, Sadie, were numbered among the most gracious hosts of the gilded age, with lavish homes in Wilmington, Newport and New York City. It is conjectured by some that these, indeed, were the "Joneses" of the expression "keeping up with the Joneses."

So, when a "bungalow" was built at Pembroke Park, it was something more than a modest hunting lodge. Jones was persuaded by friend and famous architect, J. Stewart Barney, to create an imposing pavilion that crowned a bluff overlooking a broad salt marsh.

Though the Jones lodge no longer stands, its large Palladian windows and sweeping staircase inspired those features in the first Landfall clubhouse.

Age-old beauty can also be seen in Landfall's reverence and preservation of the natural environment, so that, in many areas, the land looks much like it did 400 years ago.

And, on an even larger scale, the entire Jones legacy of understated elegance, hospitality and relaxed grace is what set the tone for today's Landfall developers.

Today, Landfall is over 2,000 acres divided among homesites, golf and recreation and wildlife preservation. As a private community, Landfall features a variety of homes and homesites options and unmatched golf, tennis, and social amenities. Landfall is the only private community in the world to offer Pete Dye and Jack Nicklaus designed golf courses. The Tennis/Swim/Fitness Center is designed by tennis great Cliff Drysdale and features grass, soft and all-weather tennis surfaces as well as a swimming pool complex, weight training and aerobics rooms.

To learn about living at Landfall call 1 (919) 256-6111.

LINDE GASES of the SOUTHEAST, INC.

During World War II, Dewitt and Eugene Merritt along with a brother-in-law, Paul Holland, worked in the welding department of a local shipyard. This was the beginning of what resulted in a long and successful business relationship with Linde, a division of Union Carbide and the supplier of industrial gases and welding equipment and supplies to the shipyard.

It was in the fall of 1946, that these three opened their doors as Merritt-Holland Company, a distributor of Linde Gases and Welding Equipment. Merritt-Holland was the first supplier of industrial gases and welding equipment to the area. In 1958, the Sunnyvale Drive plant began producing oxy-gen and acetylene in a 7,800 square foot building on a 4 acre lot. In 1987 the company acquired 4 acres of adjoining land and more than tripled the plant operation in square footage. Today this state-of-the-art plant and laboratory supplies a wide spectrum of high purity gases and gas mixtures to a diverse group of Wilmington industries, as well as oxygen and acetylene to the backyard mechanic.

By 1974, when the company was acquired by Linde, it had grown from its one Wilmington location to 14 locations throughout the Carolinas. Since the acquisition the company continued to expand with operations in South Carolina and Tennessee. Most recently the company acquired Wolfe Welding Supply, a welding distributor in Atlanta, Georgia. The company now services 20,000 customers from 18 locations in the Carolinas, Georgia and eastern Tennessee. The location at 1902 Dawson Street remains the corporate headquarters and base for one third of the company's 250 employees.

In October of 1988 Merritt-Holland Company changed its name to Linde Gases of the Southeast to more closely align itself with its parent company and support its plans for growth throughout the southeast. Linde Gases of the Southeast is working to do things better today than yesterday and still better tomorrow.

LOWRIMORE, WARWICK & CO.

Seated from left to right: Samuel R. Rose III, W. Michael Clewis, and David R. Ward; Standing from left to right: Robert F. Hutchens, J. Mark Stanley, Robert F. Warwick (Managing Partner), and T. Alan Phillips.

Lowrimore, Warwick and Co. was started by C. S. Lowrimore in 1941. The current managing partner, Robert F. Warwick, joined the firm in 1958, and became managing partner in 1973 when Lowrimore retired.

Since 1973, the firm has grown from one office and 12 employees, to three offices and 80 employees, eight of whom are partners. The Wilmington office moved in 1985 from its location in the Cotton Exchange to its current location in the newly renovated Warwick Building. The building, which is in the heart of Wilmington's downtown business district, faces Grace and Front streets and wraps around the existing Efird Building. The two additional locations, Greenville and Whiteville, were carefully chosen based on the need in those areas for the services that Lowrimore, Warwick & Co. can provide.

In 1973, Warwick and the other three partners made a decision that the firm would specialize in specific areas— Audit and Accounting, Tax, Small Business and Management Advisory Services. These areas of specialization still

exist today, although some of the titles have changed to reflect current terminology. The Small Business Department is now Business Management Services and Management Advisory Services is entitled Management Information Systems.

Lowrimore, Warwick & Co. has a comprehensive Medical/Dental Practice Management Group, which provides services for doctors and dentists in all areas of tax and accounting, as well as management of individual practice units. The firm also has a Financial Institutions Services Group that provides consulting services to banks, savings and loans and other financial institutions. Another major field of service is financial planning, an area in which the firm has been very aggressive. Their services include income tax planning, retirement planning, risk management, investment analysis, financial counseling and estate planning.

In 1975, Lowrimore, Warwick & Co. joined the Association of Regional Accounting Firms, the largest association of regional CPA firms in the United

States, which allows the firm to access a wide range of expertise and ideas from 60 member accounting firms in 37 states and Canada. Other associations that the firm remains active in include the SEC Practice Section; the Private Companies Practice Section of the American Institute of CPA's; and NR International, an international association of CPA firms with representation throughout the industrialized world, with Mr. Warwick as a director.

Involvement in its community is vital to any company. Mr. Warwick served as chairman of the Committee of 100 (industrial development) from 1983-84, and president of the Chamber of Commerce from 1980-81. The firm as a whole is active with the local Azalea Festival as well as the United Way Campaign and other community projects. The philosophy of Lowrimore, Warwick & Co. is found in its client brochure: "As a neighbor and a member of the same business community, we are directly concerned with the success of our clients. Our plans are to continue to grow with our clients."

LOWE'S OF WILMINGTON

Lowe's Companies, Inc., originally known as North Wilkesboro Hardware, was founded in 1921 by L. S. Lowe. In 1940, L. S. Lowe's daughter, Ruth Lowe, sold North Wilkesboro Hardware to her brother James L. Lowe for $4,200. She married H. Carl Buchan, Jr., who was then employed in the traffic department of the Atlantic & East Carolina Railroad. Buchan proceeded to assume management of the company and direct it to enormous growth. He continued to work for the railroad until 1942, when he enlisted in the Army. Mr. Lowe joined the Air Corps while Mrs. Buchan and her mother operated North Wilkesboro Hardware. After Carl Buchan's death, Lowe's new management team continued to expand the company.

Lowe's opened its twenty-ninth store in Wilmington, North Carolina, on August 4th, 1964 in the old Smith Building Supply building which housed approximately 5,000 square feet of retail selling space. Bill Cothren had come from Raleigh to manage the Castle Hayne Road store with its eighteen employees. At that time, the hourly wage Lowe's paid was $1.25. In 1968, Bill Cothren retired from Lowe's Companies and Bob Tillman became the new manager. One of Bob's more colorful memories is

that of the alligators behind the store that entered the lumber yard during the winter to lie in the sun. This complication scared more than one or two of the warehousemen!

In 1974, Lowe's decided to move to its current location. A larger store of 12,000 square feet was built. Ten years later the store doubled in size, bringing its retail selling up to 24,000 square feet. For Bill Pelon, store manager since March of 1985, and the 110 other employees, 1989 will be a banner year since it will mark Lowe's 25th year in the Wilmington area as well as the opening of a new 60,000 square foot store.

The revolutionary idea that led to Lowe's rapid growth was buying directly from manufacturers at the same prices that wholesalers were paying, and to sell to the general public at the same prices the dealer had to pay. This is one of the many reasons that Lowe's remains the nation's largest lumber and hardware supply retailer. An innovation that has been initiated by Lowe's is the Home Design Alternatives Customizer System. It allows customers to pick from the most popular home designs today and modify the home design they choose exactly as they want it. The blueprints and a material list of the items needed

to build the chosen home can be provided by Lowe's along with a single total cost of the materials. Lowe's guarantees the total cost will not change for 90 days after the commitment to buy.

Along with the many obligations that are involved in running a business, several executives have played important roles in key civic and state affairs. Bob Tillman, senior vice-president of merchandising Lowe's companies, served as president of the Greater Wilmington Merchant Association as well as president of the Wilmington Chamber of Commerce. Robert L. Strickland, chairman of the board, served as a member of the North Carolina House of Representatives, from 1962 to 1964. Leonard G. Herring, president and chief executive officer, serves as director of the Governor's Business Council on Arts and Humanities, Inc., as well as a member of the University of North Carolina Board of Visitors.

Lowe's Companies plans to build 150 new stores over the next three years ranging in size from 40,000 to 100,000 square feet of retail selling space. Lowe's currently has over 300 stores with sales in excess of 2.7 billion dollars.

N.C. STATE PORT AUTHORITY

ing the past three decades more than thirtyfold. The NCSPA promotes international trade and economic development through its offices in Wilmington, Morehead City, Charlotte, New York City, London, Dusseldorf, Seoul, Tokyo, and Hong Kong. Ships flying flags from over 200 ports of call sail in and out of North Carolina Ports annually.

At Wilmington, the terminal is located 26 miles from the mouth of Cape Fear River. The channel and turning basins are maintained at a depth of 38 feet. A marginal wharf of 6,040 feet with double railroad tracks assures shippers and receivers rapid and efficient cargo handling. Storage facilities include 1.5 million square feet of sprinkler-equipped interior space and 130 acres of paved exterior area.

Three 40-ton full-bridge container cranes and additional gantry and mobile cranes are used to load and unload ships at the dock. The CSX Railroad and over 50 motor carriers provide inland transportation to and from the facility. Tonnage at Wilmington alone reached 3.5 million last year which was an all-time record. The entire State Port of Wilmington has been designated a Foreign Trade Zone offering warehouse and storage for use as a special customs trade zone.

The NCSPA also offers services at two inland container storage and staging areas in Charlotte and Greensboro. These two facilities were the first port-operated inland ports to be established in the United States offering reduced shipping rates for importers and exporters wishing to use North Carolina's ports.

The NCSPA is in the midst of the largest capital expansion program in its history with over $36 million in projects underway at both port facilities. The centerpiece of this program is a giant 900-foot container berth at Wilmington which will be completed during the summer of 1989. Two new container cranes will be added to the berth for cargo handling in December 1989.

To be completed this fall will be two comprehensive marketing feasibility studies at each port to give the NCSPA a master strategy for developing and maintaining North Carolina's ports through the next decade. Another ports' expansion and maintenance program is also being reviewed by the NCSPA's board of directors for 1990.

During the 1920s, farsighted citizens of North Carolina saw the need for development of deep water ports at Wilmington and Morehead City and they approached the State Legislature for support. Federal assistance from the U.S. Army Corps of Engineers kept channels dredged and the harbors clear. During World War II, the harbor and shipyard at Wilmington played a major role in the production of cargo ships to carry war supplies and troops throughout the Atlantic and Pacific.

As a result of the port's participation during the war and the development of port facilities, the North Carolina State Ports Authority was created by the General Assembly in 1945. It was commissioned to contribute to the economic growth of the state through development and maintenance of modern and efficient port facilities at Wilmington and Morehead City.

A 1949 law further defined the job of the NCSPA to develop and improve the harbors and seaports of North Carolina for a more expeditious and effective handling of water-borne commerce to and from any place or places in the state and other states and foreign countries.

Today manufactured goods and raw materials from around the world enter and leave the United States through North Carolina's state-owned deep water ports. Last year a record 8 million tons was handled through the facilities on over 1,000 ships.

The citizens of North Carolina are the shareholders in this governmental entity, which has increased tonnage dur-

NEW HANOVER MEMORIAL HOSPITAL

New Hanover Memorial Hospital was conceptualized in the early 1960s by a group of community leaders who organized a New Hanover County Hospital Authority. This group, in assessing area medical facility needs, determined that both of the existing hospitals were antiquated and obsolete and that Wilmington and the New Hanover County area were in need of a modern, up-to-date acute care hospital.

Actual construction of New Hanover Memorial Hospital (NHMH) was begun in early 1963 at a site on South 17th Street within the City of Wilmington, which was approved by the county voters. The hospital opened in mid-1967 with a complement of 404 acute care beds and a medical staff which numbered 100 physicians by the end of the year.

By the early 1970s, NHMH had developed as a major healthcare resource. Through an agreement with the University of North Carolina Medical School, NHMH became a site for clinical training for medical students and medical residents, and an Area Health Education Center (AHEC) was established. This designation lead to the construction of staff quarters at the rear of the hospital in 1971 to house personnel training at NHMH. In 1974, using a combination of grant funds and local contributions, the Cameron Education Building to house the AHEC Program was completed adjacent to and connecting with the main hospital.

As a result of increased patient care service and teaching function expansion at NHMH through the mid-1970s, New Hanover County voters approved an expansion of the hospital in 1974. This expansion project included the addition of three floors to the patient care tower, expansion and relocation of critical care areas, expansion of outpatient clinic areas, other support and ancillary services, and parking. The NHMH major expansion project was completed in 1981, adding three floors to the patient tower, and doubling the area of the maintenance and service floors.

Currently, NHMH has a licensed bed capacity of 568 beds and a medical staff of 256 physicians, representing over 28

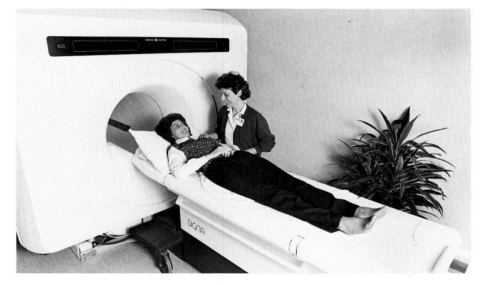

medical specialties and subspecialties. The hospital serves a seven-county area offering a full array of healthcare services which include: open heart surgery and cardiac catheterization; magnetic resonance imaging (MRI); neonatal intensive care; a family centered obstetrical unit and an innovative and highly acclaimed freestanding psychiatric facility, The Oaks.

The growth of New Hanover Memorial Hospital has led to its recognition as a major asset and attraction for business and industry moving into Southeastern North Carolina. New Hanover County citizens and hospital employees alike take pride in the fact that New Hanover Memorial Hospital truly represents "the State of the Art of Caring."

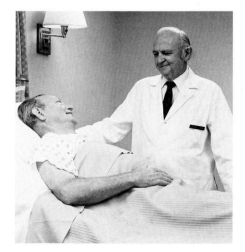

NOFFSINGER, INC., REALTORS®

Noffsinger, Inc., REALTORS® was founded in 1962 by Hugh Godwin Noffsinger, Jr.

A native of Richmond, Virginia, Noffsinger is a graduate of the University of Richmond with a Masters Degree in Business Administration from Harvard University. The company was founded to provide general real estate services with a special emphasis on residential sales.

Approximately two years later, his wife Sally joined him and subsequently became president and manager of the residential sales division, as Hugh Noffsinger increasingly focused his efforts on the appraisal end of the business.

The business flourished and at various times has engaged in residential development and construction, commercial development and sales, property management, insurance, and appraisals, all the while continuing to provide a steady stream of customers with the "home of their dreams" while focusing personal attention and service to those clients whom the company represented in the sale of their property.

In early 1987, with the principals aging, controlling interest in the business was sold to A. Thomas Spencer, Jr., husband of the Noffsinger's oldest daughter, Peggy. A Wilmington native, Spencer is a veteran of twenty years in the real estate business having served as administrative vice president of the North Carolina Association of REALTORS®, executive vice president of the South Carolina Association of REALTORS®, vice president and manager of two large real estate brokerage firms in Charleston, South Carolina, and Greensboro, North Carolina, and most recently as vice president of marketing for the regional arm of a national builder/developer headquartered in Greensboro, and building in various locations across North Carolina.

Peggy N. Spencer serves as the firm's relocation director, specializing in assisting families moving to Wilmington in receiving advance information and aiding generally in whatever way may make their move more comfortable. She also works with corporations relocating employees to assist in the sale of their properties.

Hugh Godwin Noffsinger, Jr.
Founder

Serving the Wilmington area from the recently remodeled offices on Wrightsville Avenue, the firm is in a major expansion mode geared toward increasing their residential sales force with a goal of becoming number one in the market place in volume, while retaining the trademark of "personal service" which has been the firm's heritage since its inception. At publication, the firm had just announced their affiliation as an independent member broker of RE/MAX.

OLSTEN TEMPORARY SERVICES

Olsten Temporary Services of Wilmington opened in 1982 with two employees and offices in The Cotton Exchange. As part of The Olsten Corporation, this new office offered area clients the experience, expertise and resources of a national temporary services company with the knowledge, strength and entrepreneurial energy of local resident Fran Young.

Today, Olsten of Wilmington has six full-time employees and provides temporary job assignments to nearly 900 workers on an annual basis. The company has grown with the community, providing value-added service to clients through the professional custom matching of temporaries with specific job assignments.

Olsten provides qualified temporaries in a broad range of skill areas, including office services, office automation, technical, marketing accounting, light industrial and health care. And all Olsten temporaries are thoroughly interviewed and evaluated to ensure a custom match to client needs.

The Olsten Corporation was founded by William Olsten, who today serves as the company's board chairman. From a single office in New York City, the Olsten network has expanded to include over 500 locations in the United States, Canada, and Puerto Rico. Its offices serve some 90,000 client accounts, and annually employ over 300,000 temporaries.

In 1986, Olsten of Wilmington purchased the Grant-Bellamy House in the city's Historic District. The home was restored and became the local Olsten office the following year. A second office in Kinston was opened in March 1984.

Rapid business expansion in Wilmington has accelerated Olsten's growth here as well. The firm, known for its commitment to service and its ability to meet client-company temporary personnel needs, maintains its position as an industry leader through the individual efforts of dedicated professionals such as Fran Young.

In addition to her business activities, Fran Young is deeply committed to the community and has served on the board of directors of United Way and as treasurer and campaign chairman of its annual fund-raising drive. She has also chaired the United Way Senior Aide Advisory Council and has served as director, membership chairman, treasurer, president-elect, and president of the Greater Wilmington Chamber of Commerce.

As an Olsten licensee, Fran Young is dedicated to providing her clients throughout the area with the finest in temporary personnel. As a resident, she is determined to work with others in the community to maintain the best of Wilmington's past, and make its future even brighter.

OCCIDENTAL CHEMICAL CORPORATION IN CASTLE HAYNE: ADDING COLOR TO THE WORLD

Chromite ore, soda ash and a small amount of lime are mixed and roasted in large rotary kilns at over 2000°F.

From curiosity to necessity

When chromium was first discovered in the late 1700s, it became a colorful curiosity, prized by rock collectors. Today, it would be hard to imagine our lives without chrome and chrome chemicals, since they literally color the world (the word "chromium" is derived from the Greek word for "color").

The chrome chemicals produced at Occidental Chemical Corporation's Castle Hayne complex are used to preserve and protect foundation timber, make clothing dyes color-fast and electroplate articles such as automotive trim and home appliances. The yellow center stripe down the highway contains chrome chemicals, as do many other paints and pigments. Chrome chemicals are also used in pharmaceuticals, perfumes, high quality audio and video tapes, and the leather tanning process.

The Castle Hayne facility

The state-of-the-art Castle Hayne plant, built in 1971 and acquired by OxyChem in 1986, is the largest, most hygienic, environmentally sound and technologically advanced chrome plant in the world.

The complex manufacturing process begins with the roasting of ground chromite ore and soda ash in large 240-foot rotary kilns, which heat the mixture to over 2000° F. Red sodium bichromate liquor is produced from the mixture following a series of filtration, acidification, purification and evaporation steps. Bichromate liquor can be further processed to produce flaked chromic acid.

Strategic location

Spanning a portion of a 150-acre tract near the northeast Cape Fear River, the Castle Hayne plant is strategically located near Wilmington's major port facilities. These facilities make it possible for the Castle Hayne plant to import raw materials not available locally and to ship finished chrome chemical products to ports around the world, including Europe and the Far East.

Major supplier worldwide

As one of only two chromium chemical plants in the United States, the world-class Castle Hayne facility produces a majority of the U.S. demand for chromic acid and sodium bichromate. The facility also produces more than 20 percent of the world demand for chromic acid and 12 percent of the world demand for sodium bichromate.

Occidental Chemical Corporation, a subsidiary of Occidental Petroleum, is a leading producer of electrochemicals and specialty products, plastics and resins, and agricultural products.

Headquartered in Dallas, Texas, OxyChem operates more than 50 manufacturing facilities worldwide and employs over 13,000 people.

Impact on the community

The Castle Hayne plant contributes significantly to the local, state and national economies. The current workforce of 220 full-time OxyChem employees results in an annual payroll of more than $8 million. The plant also supports the local economy by purchasing about $10 million annually in raw materials, goods and services from local manufacturers and suppliers.

OxyChem's Castle Hayne employees are also involved in making the community a better place to live and work. They participate in a variety of community activities and contribute to numerous local charitable causes.

OxyChem is glad to be part of the Wilmington community. The employees at the Castle Hayne plant salute Wilmington's 250th anniversary and look forward to a future colored with excellence.

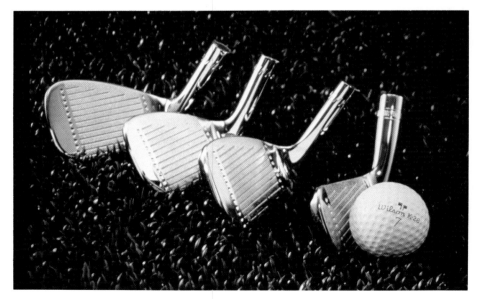

In addition to adding color to the world, chrome chemicals are used in wood preservation and metal finishing.

PLANTATION VILLAGE

Plantation Village, the first full service life-care community in eastern North Carolina, was founded on October 18, 1988 by members of the Champion McDowell Davis Foundation. Located just north of Wilmington, Plantation Village brings to residents of the Southeast North Carolina area who are aged 62 and over a way of retirement living known as continuing care or "life care." This concept offers active retirees a lifestyle which is designed to meet their unique needs while allowing them the freedom to pursue their personal interests. Life-care communities, such as Plantation Village, encompass these important components: a private, resort-oriented living unit, a wide array of personal services, health care in the Cornelia Nixon Davis Health Care Center, all combined within a sound financial plan. Plantation Village is a not-for-profit corporation which is committed to developing and managing a quality adult community which is fiscally sound and genuinely responsive to resident needs.

Plantation Village was developed and is being managed by Life Care Services Corporation (LCS), specialists in life-care and headquartered in Des Moines, Iowa. LCS is recognized as a leader in the development and management of life-care retirement communities. Since 1961 the principal officers of LCS have been instrumental in the planning, development and management of over 60 retirement communities throughout the United States. LCS and an affiliate management company are currently managing 40 life-care retirement communities similar to the Village.

The principal operating officers of LCS are Fred W. Weitz, Richard A. Wilkey and Stan G. Thurston. The principal development officers are D. William "Bill" Klemme and Steve Hoover.

Plantation Village plans to add additional apartments and villas, a health care center, and an expansion of the fine dining facilities in future phases.

SOUTH ATLANTIC SERVICES

South Atlantic Services, Inc, is a contract service company and was founded in 1971 by W. Mercer Rowe. Located on U.S. Highway 421 North, near Wilmington, the company blends, packages, and ships antifreeze, motor oils, various powders, lighter fluid, and other industrial and agricultural products for a number of major corporations.

The company also manufactures plastic containers which are used for many of the products it produces. The company has initiated a number of packaging innovations on its own and with its customers.

Rowe came to Wilmington in 1961 as president and chief operating officer, to build the Carolina Nitrogen Plant on U.S. Highway 421 North. A few years later W.R. Grace Company bought out the other investors and Rowe became Vice President of the firm. Grace suggested that Rowe move to New York; however, Rowe and his family had found a life style, people, and an area they liked and wanted to stay in Wilmington.

South Atlantic Services, Inc., offers over eighteen years of experience and specialization in contract services for industrial companies. Starting with only one customer, the company has served many of the blue chip companies of America...the likes of DuPont, Union Carbide, Texaco, TENNECO, PPG Industries, FMC Corporation, and Chevron.

The Wilmington plant site has grown from 50,000 square feet to 240,000 square feet.

In 1980, the company established a plant in Atlanta, Georgia, at the request

of several of its customers. This successful expansion prompted the company to relocate its Atlanta facilities to Panama City, Florida, in 1987 to take advantage of low cost water transportation for major raw materials. The modern Florida plant is located in a 90,000 square foot building which in addition to its other operations, contains a blow-molding plant to supply its customers with plastic containers.

The nature of the contract packaging business is that the packager develops a necessary close operational relationship with its customers. In many instances the company supplies the raw materials used to produce the customer's product. In other instances the company's customers supply raw materials, maintaining at the company's premises an inventory of packaged products ready for distribution.

In addition to a heavy business schedule, Rowe has always found time for his civic interests. He has served as president of the Chamber of Commerce as well as trustee of Cape Fear Community College for twelve years. Rowe is also a member of the North Carolina Department of Transportation Aviation Council and the Lower Cape Fear Water and Sewer Authority for eight years.

WILMINGTON SHIPPING COMPANY

Founded on November 13, 1945, Wilmington Shipping Company was a direct outgrowth of the Wilmington Terminal Warehouse Company, the major waterfront terminal at the time. Members of the Sprunt family, owners of the Wilmington Terminal Warehouse Company, and Peter Browne Ruffin, William Parsley Emerson, and Worth D. Williams created the steamship agency and stevedoring organization to complete the successful terminal operations already in existence. Acting as agents for the Maritime Administration's reserve fleet of ships on the Brunswick River, the Wilmington Shipping Company grew tremendously in its first year.

The business was carried on jointly between the two companies until 1953, when a fire completely destroyed the facilities of the Wilmington Terminal Warehouse Company. As it was not feasible to rebuild the Wilmington Terminal Warehouse—the North Carolina State Ports Authority was just completing the State Port Terminals—the Wilmington Terminal Warehouse Company was dissolved, and Wilmington Shipping Company continued.

In 1954, the company moved again, this time into new offices in the Administration building of the State Ports Authority. Offices were maintained there until 1963, when the building was torn down in order to make way for a new storage warehouse. Wilmington Shipping Company then occupied temporary quarters on South Front Street until the new Ports Authority Building was completed. That space was occupied for thirteen years until the company moved into the present location on Shipyard Boulevard in 1978.

Early on, Morehead City was seen as increasingly important in the export and import future of North Carolina. Accordingly, Morehead City Shipping Company was established as a branch office in February 1954. The Wilmington and Morehead City companies originally acted as steamship agents and stevedores, and subsequently, licenses were obtained to act as customhouse brokers and freight forwarders. This four-fold approach continued until 1969, when the customhouse brokerage and freight forwarding activities were placed under a new corporate entity, Southern Overseas Corporation, a wholly-owned subsidiary of Wilmington Shipping Company.

Growth and expansion have occurred since. An office of Wilmington Shipping Company was established in Charlotte in August 1964, and further expansion occurred as new Southern Overseas Corporation offices were established in Norfolk in July 1969, in Charleston in July 1974, and in Savannah in September 1985. All of these offices continue to be active. In 1968, East Carolina Ship Agencies, Inc., another wholly-owned subsidiary of Wilmington Shipping Company, was organized. East Carolina operates in Wilmington and Morehead City, and represents a number of well-established lines in various trades. Since 1987, it has owned and operated East Carolina Bonded Warehouse on River Road in Wilmington.

In 1985, Wilmington Shipping Company purchased the assets of Chestnut Enterprises and entered the container depot and maintenance and repair business on Carolina Beach Road and at the State Port Terminals. In 1987, the company formed Chestnut Enterprises Trucking with 48 state interstate operating authority. This facility is located on River Road.

Wilmington Shipping Company's plans for future development are to continue its present activities and modernize equipment and methods to meet the continuing challenges of ever-changing conditions in world trade and distribution.

BIBLIOGRAPHY

Edmonds, Helen. *The Negro and Fusion Politics in North Carolina.* Chapel Hill, N. C.: The University of North Carolina Press, 1951.

Hall, Lewis. *Land of the Golden River, Volume One.* Wilmington, N. C.: The Wilmington Printing Company, 1975.

Hall, Lewis. *Land of the Golden River, Volumes Two and Three.* Wilmington, N. C.: The Wilmington Printing Company, 1980.

Hewlett, Crockette. *Between the Creeks.* Wilmington, N. C.: The Wilmington Printing Company, 1971.

Howell, Andrew J. *The Book of Wilmington.* Wilmington, N. C., 1930.

Lee, Lawrence. *The Lower Cape Fear in Colonial Days.* Chapel Hill, N. C.: The University of North Carolina Press, 1965.

Lennon, Donald R. and Kellam, Ida B. *The Wilmington Town Book.* Raleigh, N. C.: North Carolina State Archives, 1973.

MacMillan, Emma W. *Wilmington's Vanished Homes and Buildings.* Raleigh, N. C.: Edwards & Broughton Company, 1966.

McKoy, Henry Bacon. *Wilmington, N. C.—Do You Remember When?* Greenville, S. C.: Keys Printing Company, 1957.

Moore, Louis T. *Stories Old and New of the Cape Fear Region.* Wilmington, N. C.: The Wilmington Printing Company, 1956.

Sprunt, James: *Tales and Traditions of the Lower Cape Fear.* Wilmington, N. C: LeGwin Brothers, 1896.

Storm, W. W. *Wilmington, Where the Cape Fear Rolls to the Sea.* n. p., n. p.

Williams, Isabel M. and McEachern, Leora H. *Salt—That Necessary Article.* Wilmington, 1973.

INDEX

Anne Russell sits on the porch of the Carolina Yacht Club. A member of a seven-generation Wilmington family, she spent holidays at Wrightsville Beach as a child. Her writing career began when she won the New Hanover High School Scribbler's Club annual contest, and many of her works are set in Wilmington. Her play *The Porch* was chosen best of show at the Cincinnati Theater Festival and was performed by The Playwrights Fund of North Carolina. She authored *Portraits of Faith*, a pictorial history of North Carolina religions, and scripted *The Talented Tenth*, a video documentary of Cape Fear black history.

Holding a PhD in American Studies, Anne Russell is an associate professor of journalism at Atlantic Christian College. She is a former entertainment editor of the Raleigh *News and Observer* and was Raleigh's first director of the arts. She lives near Wrightsville Beach in a house designed by her architect husband Howard Reed Garriss, and she is the mother of four daughters. Photograph by Dick Parrott.